*Good words are expen
cost in full. Her life is m
and an unrelenting desi..................
life. She hands us a compass to seek the same.
'Whole' is a gift to be read, received and passed on.*
**Joshua Luke Smith,
Poet, Writer, Musician, Podcaster**

*Olivia's book offers a vibrant vision for living with
open-hearted curiosity about our place and purpose
in the world. Drawing on wisdom from her Christian
faith and many other rich sources, she guides the
reader towards profound insights and accessible
practices to support wellbeing and resilience
whatever life may bring.*
**Belinda Norrington,
Mindfulness Teacher at Wild Acre Wellbeing**

*This is a book of profound wisdom...cultivated on a
personal journey that has encountered suffering,
trauma and shock and yet the author has been
remade through it. In that remaking, she has faced
reality with a wise embodied spirituality.
This book offers hope to all who find themselves
reconstructing their world.*
**Revd Dr Shaun Lambert,
Mindfulness Chaplain at The Scargill Movement**

*'Whole' is very well written providing helpful
practices for opening the body, soul and mind
toward wholeness. The author's personal
experiences, Christian faith and wisdom add depth
to the book. As a Christian yoga instructor, I find that
this book contains much wisdom
I can share with my students.*
Rie Skårhøj, Founder of CrossYoga

WHOLE

A pathway to peace and fulfillment

Contents

Chapter 4: Everyday Graces

Introduction
Breathing
Moving
Eating
Cleansing
Clothing

Chapter 5: Sacred Bodies

Introduction
Embodiment
Physical Senses
Inner Sensing
Posturing
Holy Whole

Chapter 6: Spiritual Earth

Introduction
Ground
Water
Greenery
Animals
Seasons

Chapter 7: Transforming Suffering

Introduction
Mystery
Stress

OLIVIA SHONE

Introduction

Can you think of a time you felt content and full of joy?

You might answer the question with a fabulous feast at Christmas with friends, or you might be painfully scanning the recesses of your memory to find any moment at all. I'll share one of my moments that occurred amid a difficult time a couple of years after my husband became blind from brain tumour surgery. Life was still incredibly intense, but seeking a short holiday, I collected the four kids straight from school on a Friday afternoon and drove us all to the seaside picking up some BBQ food along the way. We went straight to the beach and burned the sausages and dropped them in the sand, as is the way, and then the kids went to play in the waves. They were laughing and splashing together as the sun set behind them. As I sat with my dear husband, both of us exhausted from our different challenges, I nonetheless experienced deep joy. This joy arose from the beauty of the beach in the setting sun, our precious children playing happily together, and a grateful acceptance that I had done well to get us all here. Sitting in the evening light watching the scene, I knew this was a moment to remember. Despite my fatigue, the big losses our family had experienced and my unresolved grief and high-stress levels, I felt peace and fulfilment at that moment. I had a sense of wholeness.

The opposite of feeling whole is feeling unfulfilled, overwhelmed and disconnected; this experience of brokenness is woven into the fabric of our daily lives, where the world feels unstable, and we experience confusion and anxiety, to name just a few of the difficult emotions we encounter. Sometimes, we feel this brokenness acutely, while at other times, we manage to cope by putting on a brave face. Our culture talks about a mental health crisis, but I believe this description is too narrow and, at times, too extreme for the experiences many of us have. We might hesitate to claim we are in crisis, as we are managing, at least outwardly. It's not just our minds that are in turmoil; our emotions are affected too, and we may experience bodily pain or even numbness connected to our stress. As for our souls, we don't have a moment or a clue how to address our spirituality as we are simply trying to survive our everyday lives. The diagnoses are narrow and extreme, and mainstream interventions are piecemeal, treating individuals as disconnected parts rather than as a holistic entity.

Despite the various challenges we face and the sense of brokenness we may feel, there is still hope for experiencing wholeness. The Old English word "*hal*" is the root of healing, health, whole and holy; these four words aptly describe what wholeness is, although a re-evaluation of the word holy is essential. Firstly, becoming whole means embracing all aspects of ourselves, valuing not only our minds and emotions but also recognising that we are spiritual and somatic (bodily) beings. To become more whole, we must engage fully with our mental, emotional, spiritual and somatic capacities, but particularly our connection with our bodies and spiritual lives. Discovering a holistic way to navigate this challenging and fractured world can foster connection and wholeness.

Building on our own holistic existence, we must also consider the whole of life. Firstly, this means addressing our own full experience of life, including our struggles and sufferings, rather than ignoring or avoiding them. Let's not go there is a refrain I've often heard, and let's pretend, is a game I frequently observe. We naturally avoid pain and challenge, so exploring these aspects of our lives can feel daunting. The irony is that when we confront our hidden pain, there is potential for transformation. Secondly, we need to realise that wholeness involves connections with all aspects of life around us, from everyday activities and relationships to our connection with nature and the Divine. This is where having a vibrant spirituality is so vital. Engaging with the entirety of life helps us discover this sense of wholeness.

As we begin to live more holistically, exploring the whole of our lives and the rich world we inhabit, we can find the peace and fulfilment we seek. The path to wholeness is as straightforward as that. This way of living transitions us from mere existence to a fuller experience of life. The Greeks had two words for life: "*bios*", from which we derive the term "biology", which represents our physical existence, or what we might call survival. The other word is *"zōē"*, like the girl's name, which describes a richer, more fulfilling way of living that we can equate with thriving. Don't we all desire to lead a peaceful and flourishing life rather than merely exist, to thrive instead of just survive, to experience wholeness instead of brokenness?

The good news is that "the life you long for is hidden in the life you are already living" as poet Joshua Luke Smith often encourages his audiences. I am passionate about exploring and helping others to live fully in the life they are already living. Living fully is about living with peace as a companion and being resilient in the face of brokenness and yet still finding enjoyment and peace in this life. This is wholeness.

My personal history has been marked neither by intense trauma nor remarkable success, which is the case for many of us. On the surface, I have led a conventional, everyday life involving family, friends and work on one hand. However, on the other hand, I have faced significant challenges and stress related to my husband, James' health. In 2012, he was diagnosed with a benign yet extensive and life-threatening brain tumour. He underwent two major brain surgeries and spent three months in hospital, including time in the intensive care unit, followed by six weeks of radiotherapy. These interventions left him almost completely blind and suffering from chronic fatigue, alongside neurological and hormonal challenges. By the end of 2013, he had lost his health, and his job and we had to leave our home, which was tied to his previous workplace. We faced an uncertain future, with no home and riddled with financial instability and four young children to consider. I describe this season as a midlife crisis of note. The challenges haven't ended either as James's health was further compromised in 2024 when he suffered a series of small strokes, one of which caused a fall from a first-floor window, resulting in another month in hospital. Consequently, he needs much more assistance, and further strokes and the remaining tumour threaten his existing health and life expectancy.

While my husband has gone through extreme suffering, this journey has impacted me in very considerable ways too. It has been an overwhelming, perplexing and painful experience in a shifting landscape. Yet, it has also been compelling as I've learnt to move beyond mere survival to genuinely thrive. I have realised that my experience of brokenness can serve as a chance for transformation, and my life is now much richer and more whole than it was 13 years ago. I can confidently say that I love my life—both my everyday life and myself—and have discovered ways to find peace and flourishing. I am passionate about pursuing a life of wholeness where peace and fulfilment are possible and sharing this with others through my work. In addition to my personal experience, my academic background in theology, training in movement, mindfulness and psychotherapy, I will also draw on the research of others to inform the pathway to wholeness offered here.

This book's narrative frame is derived from my own experience and those of countless women the world over. Bringing a redemptive lens to women's experience offers us guiding principles on the pathway to wholeness, which each chapter will explore. The aim is to offer a counterbalance to a Western interpretation that has often perceived wellbeing and spirituality from the perspective of men. However, this pathway to wholeness is available for everyone. It recognises the cultural beliefs shaped by centuries of male dominance without it being an indictment of men. Whoever you are and whether you consider yourself spiritual, seeking or stressed and struggling, you are able to find personal wholeness in a broken world. The journey begins with the life you are currently living, to explore its internal landscape with curiosity and courage, to uncover the hidden treasures within.

The pathway to wholeness is neither linear nor progressive, so you can begin anywhere in the book-whether at the start or by dipping in and out. Each chapter focuses on a different aspect of women's experiences, with subsections offering somatic-spiritual practices for exploration and experimentation. I recommend reading it slowly and reflectively, perhaps even reading just one section per day, and engaging in the practices, which are resources you can revisit anytime. These practices blend contemporary somatic wellbeing approaches although breath and body awareness may be triggering or unhelpful for some, so use the practices only as you find beneficial. The spirituality offered draws from the enduring wisdom of the Christian tradition. Whilst this might initially deter some folk, I encourage curiosity and a relinquishing of bias against this religion, as it is appropriate here through a more feminine lens.

'Whole' aims to guide the reader toward a fully embodied way of living that encompasses our body, mind, heart and soul, allowing us to lead a life rich in healing, health, wholeness and even holiness.

Let's explore with curiosity, engage with courage and experience through contemplation a way to become whole that brings peace and fulfilment to our daily lives.

OLIVIA SHONE

Chapter 1

Hidden Treasure

'Invisible Women' by Caroline Criado Perez shares numerous stories and statistics about how women have been ignored, forgotten and hidden in various areas of domestic and public life around the globe. Indeed, millions of women have been concealed behind closed doors, excluded from mainstream education or public platforms, or have had their importance diminished by others. As women gain a voice, they can provide insights based on their experiences. Being invisible is a common experience for many women, and each of us has hidden aspects of our own lives. Perhaps we have felt completely overlooked and unimportant, or rather that there are parts of ourselves or our stories that remain hidden. Maybe it's time for you to explore and uncover the hidden aspects of your life to see if there might be something valuable within them.

I'm a jeweller's daughter, and growing up, I've seen many beautiful and precious gems. My father would regularly open his briefcase and hold out a large, single stone, like a fancy pink diamond or a deep blue sapphire, in his palm for me to approve or place a glittering diamond necklace around my neck to see what I thought. The precious things in life, like jewels, originate from the earth, where they are hidden and need excavation and polishing. There are treasures hidden within your own life that are waiting to be discovered to become polished and glittering gems that adorn your everyday existence.

Becoming whole involves discovering the hidden jewels of your life that may initially seem grubby and unappealing. Whilst getting our hands dirty with the raw materials of life isn't immediately attractive, it often leads to precious and beautiful outcomes. The treasures of healing, health and wholeness are embedded in the life you are already living, so you don't need to search elsewhere to find them. The gift of wholeness is not found out there somewhere but within the ground of your own life, in who you are, right here, right now.

The spiritual realm operates according to the rule of hidden treasures if we can name it as such. Having studied the Bible, God and spiritual experience, I can say without doubt that the good spiritual things are hidden. My own Christian tradition reveals a hidden God. He isn't easily known and we have to search out his reality as he isn't writing his name in the sky with fireworks or rendering doctors redundant with regular miracles at local hospitals. Christ, "in whom are hidden all the treasures of wisdom and knowledge," (Colossians 2:3), was concealed for centuries and when Jesus finally came to earth, He was obscured for thirty years in a Roman outpost. He attempted to hide His true identity when He was released into His ministry, opting to teach His listeners by hiding the truth in parables. In His dying moments, Jesus cries out to His Father, "Why have you forsaken me?" revealing that even the Son of God finds the Father to be hidden. On the surface, it seems insane! Why would God hide Himself so much?

The answer lies in the seeking and the finding. Whether you're seeking to live more fully, know yourself better, or understand God, you'll discover treasure if you seek it out in the hidden places. The pathway to wholeness can provide the confidence to venture into the unknown, even if it feels a little daunting. Here, you will find a stronger, truer, richer and more beautiful sense of self, the world and even the Divine.

The Unknown

Do you lean more towards curiosity or fear in the face of the unknown?

When we turn toward what is hidden, we can adopt two attitudes. The first is fear, which seeks to protect us from the unknown by expecting the worst and drawing back. But an alternative attitude is curiosity which can lead us forward into discovery.

Famous pioneers can teach us how to venture into the unknown. The European explorers who sailed into the unchartered world captured my attention during childhood. I'm sure they had fears, and I imagine they had to convince sponsors and crew that their ships would not sail off the edge of a flat earth or be marooned forever at sea; that they would reach land safely before food ran out or the ship was wrecked on unknown islands. Similar bravery and enquiry were demonstrated by the scientist Marie Curie, who waded through tons of pitchblende, risking radiation exposure to make groundbreaking discoveries in radioactivity. The courage and curiosity of these pioneering explorers outweighed their fears, allowing them to investigate the unknown to discover valuable things.

If we believe treasure exists, we can more readily choose courage and realise that the ghosts and ghouls are often just that—insubstantial or illusory concerns that hold far less substance than the gold we are seeking. Exploring the unknown dimensions of ourselves, our relationships, our lives and the Divine requires confidence and curiosity to overcome fear. We can either retreat from the unknown in fear or approach it with curiosity.

In my half-century of living, I haven't travelled, worked, read or experienced the outer life as widely as many people. However, I have learnt what it means to live deeply within my own life. I have truly explored what it is to be me, what it means to be a mother to different children with varied needs and what it means to be a wife to a healthy, then sick, and then disabled husband. I have found treasures hidden within the life I am already living, and there is so much more to discover. It is this personal experience that has led me back into the profession of therapy, so I can walk with others along a path of discovery through the dark valleys of uncertainty and fear. Many clients show great courage and emerge stronger, more self-confident, and more connected to life as a result of the healing journey, offering contemporary witness to this potency.

My constant experience has been that I am not alone as I venture into the unknown. I have found great comfort in the promise that Jesus "will never leave us or forsake us." Knowing this enables me to explore my inner fears of worthlessness or anger, the challenge of a failing relationship or the difficulty that suffering brings to my understanding of a loving God. I can confront these unknown and threatening areas with the presence of the Divine, and hope to find the "hidden treasures, riches stored in secret places" (Isaiah) that He promises us.

Becoming whole involves exploring hidden anxieties and repressed sadness, along with our confusion and fears. By exposing these emotions, we can express and release them, allowing healing to take place. Similarly, discovering our unique, untapped gifts and characteristics can lead to fulfilment and wholeness. This pathway delves into unknown aspects of the self, relationships, the world and the Divine mystery, yet we are not alone in our quest to uncover life's hidden treasures.

------ ⚭ ------

Practice

Settle yourself wherever you are, giving yourself some moments to be quiet to contemplate.

Ask yourself: How do I feel about the unknown?

Gentle challenge: What am I hiding from today, and can I approach this with curiosity?

Be curious about whatever comes up. Hold these things in your awareness as you hold yourself with compassion.

God also holds you and your hidden concerns as you bring them into conscious awareness.

Be encouraged: Learn these words by heart to strengthen you when you find fear of the unknown rising in your heart.

"Even though I walk through the valley of the shadow of death, you are with me" (Psalm 23).

Shifting Perspective

We need to shift our perspective if we are to explore the hidden areas of our lives. Instead of looking towards the future, or the horizon of opportunity or to others, we need to make our focal point within our own existence to find the treasure.

Perspective, in artistic terms, was discovered by the early Italian Renaissance artists. They would draw faint lines from the edges of their canvas that converged at one point in the middle, denoting the far distance and making sense of everything else in their paintings. Earlier works, like Uccello's The Hunt in the Forest, were groundbreaking back in 1470, but to my 17-year-old gaze in Art History A-Level, they appeared childlike and crude. The way many of us view life resembles that of the classical artist, where we see the point of our life at a distant point out there on the horizon. We can set goals for the future by focusing on potential job opportunities, holidays, the success of our children or retirement. Sometimes, the point might be achievable and even laudable; other times, less so. However, if we only define the point of life by something out there, we might literally be missing the point.

Perspective does not only operate in the classical way, where lines converge to a distant point. There is also what we can call a divergent perspective point. As I stood in the middle of my local city, Bath, a while back and looked in all directions to test the local truth that one can always see green hills, I became aware of this. While standing and reflecting, I noticed that the lines of perspective diverged from within me. The point of perspective was in me. It was a game changer as I sensed the Spirit whispering to me, telling me that I was the point of my life and that my life didn't derive meaning from something more important out there, as if all my focus should be on reaching a destination or defining myself by something I had to achieve. Rather, I was at the point where meaning was already located. I am important and have a place in this world and a unique perspective that allows me to see things differently, which is the same truth for us all. How I see and experience the world from my subjective standpoint is actually the point or the locus of meaning for my life.

The same goes for each of us. Rather than the point being out there we are the valuable point of our own life.

Practice

Sit quietly.

Do you ever wonder what the point of your life is? As though the answer lies somewhere out there?

Bring your awareness to your body, that it takes up space, that it has a physical presence on the chair.

Narrow your awareness to your breath or to a central point within your body if you prefer.

Become aware of yourself as you breathe and are present to yourself.

Allow this embodied awareness to help you understand that you are in the here and now and that within you is the starting point to engage with meaning and wholeness.

Rich Inscape

If we are the focal point of our lives, then our life is worth exploring. As we delve into what is already present within us and engage with our everyday experiences, we can uncover the riches of insight, emotional fulfilment and transformation. The hidden, internal world is profoundly rewarding although exploration can initially be unsettling.

I remember as a teenager, like many others, how I struggled with my sense of identity. Despite achieving and checking many boxes on the surface, I was deeply uncomfortable with who I was, grappling with self-hatred and enduring a few years of mild but chronic eating disorders. A pivotal moment of healing occurred at 20 when I confessed to a visiting speaker, a Christian psychotherapist at my university, that I had an issue with food and feelings of worthlessness. Our two-hour conversation, which delved into these hidden struggles and included moments of silence, awkwardness and tears, served as a significant turning point for me. Nowadays, with an awareness of my various shortcomings, I find my existence rich and interesting, and the world around me can feel safe, beautiful and truly alive. This sense of fulfilment has emerged as I have explored and experienced my own inscape.

Perhaps you are a cynic who thinks we should all just get on with our lives. Or maybe you are an extrovert who feels bored by the idea of retreating inward. However, the desire for wholeness is neither narcissistic, negative, nor boring, as our internal world is designed to be rich and life-giving. Poet Gerard Manley Hopkins uses the term inscape— meaning an inner landscape—to describe how a thing or creature has its own innate meaning that can be explored for patterns of beauty and significance revealed through observation.

Science observes an inscape in nature, with quantum physics exploring this hidden internal world. Quantum laws and patterns are beautiful and complex and operate independently of classical physics. Turning towards the inscape of our own lives means exploring our hidden experiences with the curiosity of a scientist as we seek to uncover concealed treasures. All things possess a rich inscape, including our own lives.

Jesus placed great importance on hidden riches. He taught the religious leaders that the presence and power of the Divine are not observable over here or over there. Rather, the Kingdom of God is within you. I suggest the Kingdom of God isn't just religious speak, but rather each individual's yearning. Don't we all long for a profound experience of the presence and power of peace, strength and fulfilment? To journey into the hidden riches of our inner life means that we may also discover the presence and power of the Divine. The Christian Mystics have understood this. The Desert Father Abba Moses is credited with saying, "Go into your cell, and your cell will teach you everything." This is understood to mean that we don't have to venture out into the world to find the healing and fulfilment we seek, but it is available for discovery right where we are if we provide space and time to explore what is already present.

To become whole and experience greater peace and fulfilment, we need to explore our own rich inscape to discover the riches within ourselves, which then connects us more deeply with the broader fabric of life and the Divine.

───── ❧ ─────

Practice

Bring awareness to your breath to settle you and focus on each inhale and exhale to calm your mind.

Bring your awareness to the centre of your physical being.

Then contemplate these words: The Kingdom of God is within you.

Read these words.

Reflect on these words and what meaning they bring you.

Respond in any way you wish to these words, to yourself or to the Divine.

Rest in this knowledge.

True Self

Are you being true to yourself? When we exist within the reality of our own inscape, we are being true to ourselves.

There are many things I haven't wanted to do, considering them at odds with who I thought I was. These include being in P.R., being a teacher and becoming a Christian and a mother. I viewed these roles as based on a fixed paradigm in which I would have to think, feel and behave a certain way to fulfil that role. Becoming a mother was the hardest role to accept, as I presumed back then that it meant only ever talking about motherhood and children and would mean a complete disconnect from my own interests and identity. In my ignorance, this is how I perceived the archetypal and culturally prescribed mother as a young adult. However, I must say that being a mother has been the most wonderful experience. Not only are my kids amazing, but I've discovered that I can be essentially me in this role. I can embrace motherhood in an authentically Olivia-shaped way, just as I've also realised I can be fully myself as a Christian. I've uncovered my true self within roles that were initially unappealing and unknown.

Uncovering our true selves is one of the greatest treasures hidden within our lives. Too often, we present a false version of ourselves to the world and even end up believing that this is who we really are.

How do you show up to others as your false self? Being our false self can feel easier than being our true self as we comply with societal expectations and adapt ourselves. Many of us operate from our false self, much of the time, feeling unsure of who we genuinely are. Donald Winnicott, the psychoanalyst, explains how the false self develops as a type of defence mechanism in our younger years, serving as a way to meet external expectations by denying the real feelings that might exist. We all develop a false self, regardless of how idyllic our childhoods might have been, as we worry about expressing what we truly think and feel, fearing misunderstanding and rejection if we reveal our true selves. Revealing our true selves can feel too risky, as it leaves no option to be anything else if we cannot be accepted for who we really are.

But the true self is the only part of us that is genuinely real. Or, as Thomas Merton, the Trappist monk, explains, the false self doesn't even exist, so how can it be known by people or by God? This is a stark reality: living as our false self is not truly living. It's merely a form of existence, not the real treasure of living fully alive, fully ourselves. It's like living the "*bios*" life of mere existence, where our true characters, gifts and fullness are hidden away, meaning we cannot find wholeness and flourishing.

Oscar Wilde encourages us, "Be yourself; everyone else is taken." However, it takes courage to explore who you truly are, and even more bravery to reveal this true self to others. Nevertheless, discovering the real you, which may be concealed within, offers a wonderful inscape of riches and meaning to enjoy. Becoming whole demands the courage to explore and express our hidden depths so that our valuable and authentic selves can be known and lived out fully. This way of being enables us to find deep peace in who we are and flourish in how we live.

Practice

Feel your physical presence in the chair and bring your awareness to your breath.

Are you aware of how you project a false self? Which situations encourage your false self to perform? With whom are you your false self?

Where or with who do you feel most truly yourself?

What are some of the characteristics that make up your true self?

Can you accept and affirm your uniqueness?

You could meditate on Psalm 139's words as a truth to support your true self: "I am awesomely and wonderfully made."

Divine Image

As we embrace our true selves, something beautiful and even Divine is revealed within us.

Photographer Jamie Keith captures stunning images of street dwellers. In the dirty, unshaven photographs, we see through the grimy layers to the essence of each person. We can sense the humour, grief or longing that these individuals carry. It's as if he invites the viewer to recognize the true self of each subject. I believe that God relates to us in a similar way. I think He is genuinely searching for the Divine blueprint He has instilled in each of us, each being a unique mirror of His divinity in human form.

Original sin is a religious concept about humanity that has garnered significant attention over the centuries; however, this term does not actually appear anywhere in the Bible. In contrast, original good is a foundational principle established repeatedly in the very first chapter. Genesis states that God created the earth in the first five days and that it was good, and on the sixth day, He created humankind, male and female, in His own image and likeness; not only was it good, but it was very good.

To say that the Divine Image within each of us is completely marred or absent is incorrect. Our true selves reflect God's image, which is very good. Jesus addressed the brokenness and evil present in people, condemning it precisely because it diminishes the Divine image. I don't deny that sin and brokenness exist within us all, but there is also something very good in each of us. Like Jamie, I believe God invites us inward to discover the hidden treasure of our true selves so we can restore and refine the Divine image within us. I remember a mindfulness client saying to me, well, I'm still alive, and God made me, so perhaps I'm not all bad. When we rely on an identity given to us—the Divine image bestowed upon us simply by being human—it can carry us through low seasons and times of uncertainty about our worth. My personal journey of healing from insecurity and former self-hatred has come from realising I am made in the Divine image and that there is innate goodness within me that I can nurture and grow.

Are you aware you have goodness, the Divine image within you? Can you also see this image in others, even beyond your close family and friends, including those who may be unappealing or difficult to deal with? If we can tune into recognising the truth of a person and their Divine imprint, we will discover something beautiful, just as Jamie does in his photos. This shift will transform our disdain into acceptance, our resentment into compassion and the ugliness that is often prevalent into a richer and more beautiful way of experiencing life. The Divine image exists within us all, offering a foundational way to live from our true selves, growing in wholeness as we embrace the truth of ourselves and others.

Practice

Find a mirror. Recognise that you might have some internal resistance as you start this process but engage with curiosity and courage in this exercise.

Sit and look at yourself. See if you can go beyond the awkwardness and hold your own gaze. Do this for at least 2 minutes if you can.

As you look at your own physical self, here you see an image of the Divine Being.

Say these words, repeating as a gentle mantra: I am made in the image of God.

Rest in the truth of this experience.

As you get up and go back into your day, remind yourself often of this fact.

Chapter 2

Restorative Silence

How often do you experience silence, a silence that brings deep peace?

Silence can enable peace to pervade our lives, but silence can often feel awkward, so we quickly fill it.

Back in 2000, I found a particular job interview full of tense pauses that I filled them by agreeing to be a housemistress to 60 girls and engage in a full timetable of teaching, sports coaching and evening duties. I wasn't even a teacher, nor did I want to be a teacher. The interview was for my husband's job and I was just coming to support him as I would also live in the new school. This headmaster was skilled at using silence to invoke teachers to agree to his propositions, knowing they would want to avoid the awkward silences he created. His tactic worked with me, and I engaged in a new and challenging job as a result.

Silence can be awkward, difficult and even oppressive. Women are profoundly familiar with this kind of silence. It has been imposed upon women in churches and public spaces where they haven't been given a voice. It also happens in the home. Women are expected to maintain silence in the face of familial or cultural demands, tirelessly giving while being silent about their own needs. This imposed silencing continues to be painful and wrong, yet women remain especially attuned to silence. I have experienced the oppression of silence due to the gender stereotypes I've unwittingly adopted or had foisted upon me. For a long time, I felt compelled to remain silent about my own struggles in deference to my husband's more obvious and serious health challenges. While that is changing, I've come to accept silence and have utilised moments of imposed quiet to reflect inwardly. I have discovered that the gift of silence can also be restorative.

The opposite of silence is noise, and to avoid the discomfort that silence can create, we will fill it with audible distractions. What noise do you have around you? Perhaps it's the noise of young children, the constant music or the unavoidable sounds like persistent traffic or loud neighbours. However, noise isn't just what is audible to our physical ears. Noise encompasses anything that captures our attention. Notifications popping up on our screens or the internal ruminations whirring in our minds also qualify as noise- attention-grabbing, peace-stealing noise. This constant barrage gradually erodes our peace and energy, leaving us tired and overwhelmed. Furthermore, the noise drowns out the deeper callings in life, distracting us from exploring our inscape and restoring our true selves.

We can lean into a restorative silence that can bring peace and health.

I first learnt the value of restorative silence when my four children were young, when the solo visit to the loo, the clock striking 7 pm, or my head hitting the pillow at 10 pm marked the silent pauses in an otherwise hectic and noisy day. When James became ill, life was ultra-manic with the external noise of my children's needs and hospital visits, as well as the inner noise of my anxious and fearful thoughts. I craved silence, and one reason I smoked a daily cigarette was the stillness that secrecy provided beneath the expansive nighttime sky. I sought silence through solitude, especially outdoors, often through running, silent, wordless prayer, as well as through my daily bad habit back then. These silences were anything but awkward, oppressive, or lonely. Instead, they offered a rich presence that restored my tired body and soul.

Silence is an absence of noise, an absence of attention-grabbing memes, notifications, work pressures and other demands. But silence is not nothingness; it is rich with possibility and offers a presence of the Divine that is peace-giving and restorative.

Silence is intertwined with stillness and space, allowing us to explore our inscape, to process various aspects of our lives and to reconnect with ourselves. It also allows us to reconnect with nature, others and the Divine. Psalm 23 describes a good shepherd "leading us beside quiet waters" to restore our souls. Amen to this type of silence that revitalises our spirits—who doesn't need that? We must recognise that not all silence is awkward, oppressive or empty; rather, silence can be our ally, providing the stillness and restorative space we need to become more fully whole.

Restorative silence allows us to acknowledge our

own unspoken stories and pain; it opens up a space for healing and for wholeness to emerge. It creates a peace-filled space to reintegrate and reconnect with ourselves, the wider world and the Divine. Instead of feeling disconnected from ourselves and the wider world, merely observing our lives as if they were played out in black and white, restorative silence enables a sense of wholeness, where life is experienced in technicolour.

Our Silent Stories

We all have stories we haven't told anyone.

I'm a therapist, so I hear many stories that clients have never shared before. There is immense power in sharing our stories. I recall suggesting to one client that journaling might be a helpful way to explore some issues, and after an awkward silence, he revealed that he was very dyslexic, so he couldn't do that. He had kept this secret from everyone except his wife, and it turned out to be one of the root causes of his feelings of inadequacy, leading him to work himself into a state of burnout to compensate.

Another client sought to relieve the silent stigma he had carried regarding a pornography addiction since he was a young boy. As we explored the origins of this addiction, self-understanding and self-compassion began to replace shame, setting him on a pathway to healing.

My own story was particularly hidden from 2012 to

2013 as I was unable to fully disclose the trauma as the community, where many of my friends were located, was an educational setting where my husband James had been appointed as the incoming headteacher. To share the details of his sight loss and chronic fatigue with this community would have unsettled it. I found myself complying with the official narrative issued by the school governors that James is undergoing interventions and will be OK to take up his post as headteacher in September. I understood the reasoning but was left feeling isolated and confused as I pretended that things were OK and James was recovering well as his prognosis was uncertain for several months. However, the reality was that he wasn't OK at all and my life was falling apart as a result.

When our pain and shame are locked up in the prison of silence, for whatever reason, it is in that silence where we need to go to unlock, release and heal our pain.

Perhaps there is an acute shame surrounding the things we don't share with anyone, or perhaps we believe that telling our story—our true experiences— is uninteresting to others or seen as self-indulgent. I have certainly felt this way regarding my husband's story; I have perceived my own story as far less interesting and important, which is why I've remained silent about my experiences for many years. Maybe we think that speaking up will break cultural norms and expose us to someone's stony judgement.

Or perhaps we fear shattering the polished image we

believe others have of us, which supports our false self. There are many reasons for our silence, but as social researcher Brené Brown, points out, shame thrives in silence, secrecy and judgment, and shame is like a cancer for our souls, denying us health and wholeness.

A restorative silence reveals what is hidden in our inscapes, allowing it to be embraced with compassion and transformed into treasure.

Silence that restores us is nonjudgmental and empathetic. It allows what is present to gently surface and be embraced. Much like the treasures of the earth—precious stones and minerals—our hidden stories reside within us and need to be excavated. When they emerge, they are in the rough, like an uncut diamond. The raw material of our experiences must be examined carefully to be truly recognised so that the treasure hidden within can be processed and transformed into something beautiful. Our silent stories are the raw material that can be transformed into something beautiful.

There is an ancient story about an Israeli woman who had been bleeding for twelve years with no medical help available. She struggled silently with the shameful, societal stigma until one day, she reached out to touch Jesus' garments amid the crowds, hoping to invoke some healing in her desperation. Jesus recognised this act of bravery and commended the woman for her quiet faith. She broke her silence, revealed her need and found healing. Another biblical story tells of a woman caught in the act of adultery, whom the religious crowd condemned as deserving of the death penalty. In the silent exchange between Jesus and this woman, he refrained from condemning her but offered compassion, allowing her to leave accepted, forgiven and free.

The pathway to wholeness explores our silent, hidden stories, allowing them to surface and be held with compassion so that they might lead to healing and wholeness.

———— ∞ ————

Practice

Sit comfortably. Spend a minute bringing your awareness to your body, feeling its physical presence on the chair. Then bring your awareness to your breath, narrowing your focus.

When you are feeling settled and calm, ask yourself,

What am I silent about?

See what comes up, without making a list, but just hold silence and space for the first one or two things that come up.

Hold these things in your own awareness, without judgement, acknowledging the reality of this part of your story.

Perhaps you could find a friend or confidant with whom you could share this silent part of your experience in the next month.

Silence as Stillness

There is an essential connection between silence, stillness and space.

Can you recall the last time, or even any time, that you found yourself in a quiet place, likely alone, perhaps in nature? Maybe gazing up at an expanse of a starry sky or watching the sunset over the sea? Or perhaps a moment when you noticed there was no one else in the house, with no loud background TV or music and silence gently enveloped you? In that moment, I wonder if you could feel a stillness, a pause from the frantic pace of life.

We are all frantically busy these days. We strive to accomplish so much, and even when we are still, our minds are occupied ruminating, regretting, fretting, boasting and planning endlessly. Buddhists refer to the monkey mind to describe the restless and active nature of the human mind.

But silence can still the restless mind and anxious heart.

There is something beautifully restorative about silence and stillness. Isn't that why we naturally need to sleep for about a third of our lives? The only way our bodies and brains can re-energise is when they are not busy and bombarded with noise. Restoration and healing come through embracing silence and stillness.

We can also encounter the Divine Presence most

easily through silence and stillness. One of the most desperate times I've ever known was soon after my husband's first major brain surgery; his brain was swelling in reaction and things were critical, with the surgeon telling me, "It's all to play for," regarding his recovery which provided anything but the reassurance I needed. As I ranted and plied questions at the nurses and railed at God, I sensed Him inviting me to go outside and saying, walk with me. I understood that there was an invitation to embrace silence, as God already knew what I was experiencing. I walked for twenty minutes, holding my inner rant at bay, pacing it out with rapid steps until I arrived at a place of stillness. Sitting down on a bench, I encountered the reassuring presence of God in the stillness. Nothing had changed in the outer medical world, but something had shifted dramatically in my inner world through this experience of silence with God. I experienced a profound shift towards a peace which surpassed logical understanding as I returned to the ICU.

My mother's favourite Bible verse, which she lovingly quotes to me when I'm anxious or upset, is, "Be still and know that I am God" (Psalm 46). This kind of stillness holds us with our stress and pain, allowing us to rest and find restoration and experience greater wholeness for our body, mind, heart and soul.

Practice

Take time today to slow down.

Find a place where you can be physically still.

Rest in this physical stillness and be silent.

Be open to the Divine Presence in the silence and stillness.

Meditate on these words in seven stages saying the words quietly each time:

Be still and know that I am God
Be still and know that I am
Be still and know that I
Be still and know that
Be still and know
Be still and
Be still
Be
Rest in the stillness.

Silence as Presence

Silence is not an absence but a presence.

If you still need convincing of the benefits of silence and have reservations about it being an empty void of familiarity and worries about grinding to a lost and lonely halt, let me reassure you that silence has a rich presence.

Karl Rahner, an innovative theologian writing in the 1950s, coined the term 'everyday mysticism' to describe those common experiences when one might sense the presence of something numinous or sacred. This sensing of the Divine Presence in everyday life can arise from moments of beauty, peace, or love, such as when we feel deeply connected to our loved ones or when we encounter the sublime in the natural world. However, this transcendent Divine Presence can also be perceived during times of depression, despair, or grief, when we reach the end of our resources and discover something just beyond us, holding, reassuring, or beckoning us. These moments of 'everyday mysticism' at the highs or lows of our lives occur when our experiences are pushed to their earthly limits, to the liminal space where heaven meets earth.

This happens to me regularly these days, so I struggle to pinpoint a specific moment. However, I do recall how I began to notice this during my teens at school. I started seeking solitude to explore life's meaning and would take myself off for walks on the nearby Malvern Hills or to the Timotei Fields initially to smoke or drink a clandestine can of cider. However, the silent solitude would offer me the chance to contemplate the possibility of something more. I became deeply drawn to a numinous sense of something beyond—something transcendent—

which I now recognise as God.

Solitude, silence and slowing down to stillness can open up a space where we can begin to perceive the Divine Presence. Perhaps you've had what Rahner refers to as an everyday mystical experience, where you've sensed the presence of something sublimely beautiful, overwhelmingly peaceful or deeply comforting, yet couldn't quite put your finger on it. This can be felt in the loving gaze shared with a pet or child, or when we witness something incredible, like a sunset or a storm. However, this Presence can also manifest, as I discovered recently, at the bedside of a dying friend, where there is a sense of something beyond ourselves, reassuring us that we are not alone. At certain moments, silence and stillness can reveal an almost tangible presence, as if beauty, love and peace have a real essence of their own. I have learnt that this is God coming to meet me in the everyday as a beautiful, loving and peaceful Presence.

An ancient story tells of the prophet Elijah, who ran in fear for his life from his persecutors. As he hid in a cave, God instructed him to exit and wait for His presence as reassurance that he would be protected. First, a powerful wind blew, then an earthquake shook the surroundings, followed by a fire and Elijah wondered if God was revealing Himself in these momentous manifestations of nature. But no. Finally, God spoke to Elijah in a still, small voice. It seems that the Divine prefers to wrap Himself in quietness and stillness as a cloak for His presence.

The pathway to wholeness invites us into a silence that reveals a tangible, life-giving and peaceful presence—a Divine Presence that brings peace to the soul.

Practice

Can you bring to mind a time when you experienced 'everyday mysticism?'

Use your imaginative senses to recall it. See, hear and feel the beauty, love or comfort of that experience.

Allow for silence and open up your awareness to silence as a presence rather than an absence.

Perhaps you might perceive a sense of the Divine Presence in the practice of silence and stillness.

Sabbath Space

Perhaps silence, slowing down, stillness and space look something like Sabbath?

For centuries, Western Christian culture enforced Sabbath laws on society, limiting or prohibiting public entertainment and working hours. I remember becoming a Christian in the 1990s, and there was a strong desire among my friends and me to move away from such restrictive thinking and behaviour, viewing it as very religious and, therefore, somewhat oppressive. However, these days I'm softening toward this biblical tradition that allows for rest from everyday demands. Theologian Walter Brueggemann discusses the worldly priorities of production and consumption that we are relentlessly encouraged to embrace, where people see themselves primarily as producers and consumers. Our culture tells us that our meaning and value are found in our productivity and purchasing power. This cycle of endless work and acquisition enslaves us, leaving us exhausted, overwhelmed and empty. Isn't it time to restore a Sabbath principle in our daily lives?

The pathway of wholeness invites us back into an experience of Sabbath rest. Scientific research has discovered the existence of a circaseptan rhythm (from the Latin "*circa*", meaning "about" and "*septa*", meaning "seven"), which refers to a biological seven-day cycle observed in physiological processes such as hormone levels and immune responses. Perhaps we would benefit from reintegrating the silence, stillness and space of the Sabbath into our weekly routines. I learnt the hard way, through diagnosed burnout back in 2016, that I needed to slow down and create some space in my busy life. I was fortunate to have my children in school, and a garden shed that I converted into my personal retreat. These days, I use an outdoor chair in the garden and bundle up in a warm, enveloping coat, hat and gloves on chilly days, which provides me with a sacred space for stillness. I enjoy a solo morning cup of tea most days in this spot, and I often conclude my day with a long bath where, once again, I find solitude in the late-night stillness and silence that I cherish.

To find the rest we long for, we could slow down and embrace silence and stillness. Finding these sacred moments in our day and week allows us to be restored. They remind us that we are not merely human doings who find our purpose in doing and purchasing, but rather human beings who need silence and stillness to rejuvenate our bodies, minds and souls. Perhaps the biblical precedent is not oppressive; instead, it offers a liberating pathway to human peace and flourishing so we may find health and wholeness.

Practice

Decide upon a physical place in or near your home that you can set apart for a Sabbath experience. Is it a particular chair, sofa or floor space? Or maybe a seat outside? Is there anything that might prompt an experience of Sabbath like a hot drink, journalling, reflective music or a candle? Can you access this Sabbath Space easily and regularly?

Use this space to give yourself permission to be silent and still.

You can spend time in peaceful rest, purposeful meditation or reflective contemplation in this space.

Silence to Savour

Slowing down to be silent and still enables us to enjoy life more.

If we truly want to appreciate a concert, we sit down and give the music our full attention silently instead of talking during the performance. If we want to enjoy a good claret, we take our time to swirl the wine, smell it and then taste and savour each sip rather than gulping it down in one motion. Or, if we want to enjoy a book or film, we need to avoid multitasking by ironing or texting at the same time. A fabulous feast enjoyed slowly, is far more satisfying than a ready meal consumed in haste.

To savour experiences, we must slow down and create space to truly enjoy them. I believe it is the intention of the Divine that we might all savour and enjoy fulfilling moments of beauty, love and peace. However, unless we slow down, stop and befriend silence and stillness, these moments will evade us. We will continue on our hamster wheels of activity, forever doing but never really living. I practise mindfulness as a way of training myself to slow down, be silent and open up space. Often, my practice starts as a bit of a chore, or I might think, maybe there is something I should be doing instead of this. But as I stick with the practice, I experience the rich inscape of life. I might encounter a more genuine appreciation of the sights, sounds, smells and sensations around me or a deeper experience of peace within. Being mindfully aware of ourselves, others and the Divine Presence allows us to experience peace and fulfilment in our own mere miraculous existence in this broken yet beautiful world.

Sometimes, silence reveals our hidden pain, whilst, at other times, it offers us a sense of peace. However, Sabbath silence is ultimately meant to help us savour life. God rested from all His work on the seventh day so He could enjoy all that He created; "He saw all that He had made, and it was very good," Genesis tells us. Can you incorporate Sabbath moments of silence and stillness to appreciate both the everyday things and also the more significant aspects, like your accomplishments or key events in life? You might argue that there are too many demands or that life is too distressing, overshadowing the possibility of enjoying it. However, we can still experience peace and beauty in the everyday despite the demands and difficulty, it is not beyond our grasp out there in the future, but in the here and now. We can slow down to savour a cup of coffee, linger over the beauty of the stars at night or enjoy a quick chat with a friendly neighbour.

These moments are what somatic and trauma-informed psychotherapist Deb Dana refers to as glimmers. We need these glimmers of hope and beauty in our lives, where we can savour the good, as they help keep us balanced and hopeful. Our daily lives are filled with opportunities for these moments of meaning, but if we don't actively slow down to find and savour them, we may find our hearts and lives feeling empty, bland and shrivelled.

Silence, stillness and space characterise a whole way of living, opening up the inscape of life so that we experience peace, see the richness of life and live with more enjoyment.

————— ❧ —————
Practice

Decide to be still for five minutes today somewhere you can practice glimmer hunting.

Use your physical senses to explore and enjoy what you see, hear, maybe touch, taste or smell.

Notice what is before you.

Use your sight to appreciate beauty.

Enjoy the sounds of birdsong or your favourite music, listened to intentionally.

You might also eat or drink a favourite thing mindfully, truly savouring the flavours.

You could use your sense of smell to enjoy fresh coffee, the scent of essential oils, or the aroma of flowers.

Let any sense of gratitude and joy that you feel be something you can also enjoy.

Chapter 3

Holistic Knowing

How often do you experience mental overload?

There is so much happening in the world and in our minds that it can leave many of us feeling overwhelmed that we can struggle with our mental health. I often grapple with information overload, often self-induced, as I love information. I have had a love affair with Google for over 10 years, as it can immediately satiate my thirst for knowledge, but I'm beginning a new relationship with an even more satisfying partner, ChatGPT. My love of knowledge might explain why I have my fingers in diverse pies, as a therapist, movement and mindfulness teacher and theologian. I have a hunger for knowledge to the point where I have irritated academics and professionals with my incessant questions. I am a victim of intellectualism, as are most of us in the modern world. Intellectualism is a left-brain, cognitive and reason-based way of knowing that insists more intellectual knowledge equals a better life and is based on the ancient principles of classical learning.

The education system in the Western world is largely based on the classical model, where students are grounded in reason and logic, research and theorising, creating theses and antitheses, which the left side of the brain excels at. As men have primarily accessed formal education, they have fostered this ancient Western way of learning, which we could maybe describe as a more masculine approach to knowledge and learning. This intellectual method of learning is promoted and prioritised as the ultimate way to navigate life: be academic, achieve good grades in school, earn a degree, acquire multiple qualifications and gain intellectual knowledge through podcasts and books, all of which equates to a solid foundation for life. However, this is a limited way of knowing that doesn't necessarily foster wisdom and flourishing in life. It prioritises cognitive thinking and leads to mental overload also causing stress.

Iain McGilchrist, in his tome, 'The Master and His Emissary', on the divided brain, explains that we have come to rely on left brain processing and that we need to engage the right side of our brain more to know in a fuller way. The right side of the brain perceives the world in a whole, intuitive and integrated way where it is aware of the wider context and meaning. It is able to grasp the emotional depth of a situation, understand metaphor, symbol and story and engage empathy, intuition, the body and wider meaning to make sense of the world. Engaging the right hemisphere of the brain enables us to have a more holistic way of knowing.

A holistic understanding means using all our faculties, not just our intellect, and engaging with every aspect of daily life instead of merely collecting information about different topics. When we talk about knowing a friend, we refer to our grasp of their essence, character and individuality, rather than simply recalling facts about them. We can have both theoretical knowledge and experiential knowledge and while both hold value, achieving a sense of wholeness requires us to move beyond just intellectual insight, which can leave us feeling disconnected from real experiences. Embracing life in its entirety is the essence of wholeness.

Historically, women have had to learn outside of the classrooms and universities, being denied access to intellectual learning, so I suggest they have more experience engaging in a holistic way of knowing. Holistic understanding involves not just right-brain thinking but also forms of knowledge that go beyond the cognitive level, incorporating somatic and spiritual awareness. Our bodies embody wisdom, intuition and perception that we can access as we navigate daily living. Developing our spiritual awareness likewise expands our experience of life beyond mere functioning or achievement. Fostering spiritual awareness allows for a more complete experience of ourselves and life, which we could describe as a more whole and also more holy experience, as we may discover the Divine mystically present within these everyday moments.

Jesus never instructed his listeners to focus on scholarly learning, nor did he present his arguments in a systematic manner. Instead, he challenges the Western mind's preference for logic by employing metaphors, parables and stories drawn from everyday life, teaching Divine principles through direct interaction with people and their bodies. Perhaps we should embrace a more grounded, everyday approach to learning in the tradition of this master teacher.

The pathway to wholeness encourages a holistic way of knowing by engaging the right side of the brain as well as the somatic and spiritual aspects of our being. It invites us to explore new ways of understanding that are intertwined with the everyday, allowing us to experience greater peace and fulfilment in our lives.

Intuition

Steve Jobs said, "Intuition is more powerful than intellect." Intuition tells us things that our intellects can't perceive.

Do you trust your intuition? I remember a time when I didn't. One autumn, I needed someone to clear up our garden. I saw a gardener with his van parked nearby and asked him if he had time to help me despite a strange feeling about him that I couldn't quite explain. He had a van full of gardening equipment and was already engaged in a gardening job, so I pushed my feelings down, choosing to trust my rational mind that everything was fine. The gardener, Roy, showed up to do the job and got to work. However, he seemed eager to drink as much tea and eat as many biscuits as possible, asking me to heat up pot noodles in our microwave. He spent more time in our house than in the garden, and my kids asked who the odd man was, clearly feeling uneasy about him as well. The gardening job took much longer than agreed, but it was when I realised he had taken a shower in our downstairs bathroom that I understood the van was his home, and our kitchen and bathroom were, for him, a means of taking care of himself. I had invited an unverified person into the heart of my home with four young children and paid for a long and poorly finished gardening clear-up as I ignored my intuition.

More positively, my intuition served me well one time during a clifftop walk when I noticed a vibrant plant growing out of the rocks. Something within me sensed it might be edible. I picked a stem and, smelling its saltiness, checked it out on my smartphone plant identifying app, and discovered it was rock samphire. I carefully bit into the succulent, pointy leaf, which tasted good. I picked some more and foraged for some mussels which I took home and prepared into a meal for my kids, (who were completely unamused and refused to eat any of it!). Perhaps intuiting safe food in nature is a little risky, but we can use our intuition to sense if someone has good intentions towards us and if an environment is safe. This is a vital, innate capacity we all have and it enables us to know in a holistic way.

Intuition warns us of threats but also directs us towards the good. Can you remember a time that your gut or your body somehow directed you to something good or something bad?

We possess a rational brain capable of making sense

of things, but we also have an intuition that seems to arise from our bodies or our guts—a voice we should heed. I have a close friend and coach, Floor, who sometimes poses a question to me and, after my well-considered response, says, "Now I'm going to ask you again, but I want you to answer from your body." I have discovered that inquiring about what my body desires or listening to my gut response often yields quicker answers than the mental gymnastics I may be accustomed to. We have a means of accessing knowledge through somatic responses, gut intuition and a spiritual sense that can be tapped into if we sidestep our usual reliance on rational thought. Holistic knowledge encourages us to open up and value these broader avenues of knowing to discover the wisdom, peace and flourishing we seek.

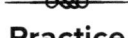

Practice

Take a moment to be silent, to be still.

Become aware of your breath.

Is there a decision you are grappling over at the moment, wondering the best way forward?

Take a minute or two for mindful awareness by tuning into your body and noticing any physical sensations you may experience.

Take a moment to consider a decision you are currently faced with.

Then, direct a question to your body and listen to the answer that rises up from within, e.g., What do you really want? Or would you prefer to do X or Y?

Listen to the answer that arises from your inner being or body rather than your brain.

It will usually present itself quite clearly. Don't get distracted by the intellectual rationalisations your mind may offer, but see if you can perceive the wisdom your body provides.

Symbol

At times, rational thinking cannot provide the wisdom and insight we require.

I recently had a client who struggled to articulate what she wanted from counselling. She attempted to provide a rational explanation but kept going off on tangents and, exasperated after 10 minutes, exclaimed, "I just can't explain it." I allowed for some silence, realising that left-brain reasoning wasn't the most helpful way for her to express her hopes for therapy. Then, breaking the silence, she explained how her friend had shown her something from the internet: a drawing of a mind full of jumbled wool, representing her state pre-therapy and another picture of a mind with discernible threads and orderly balls of coloured wool inside it. "I want that", she said. A picture can tell a thousand words. She recognised she was overwhelmed with grief and confusion, but it was the humour and symbolism of the picture that helped her understand what she truly wanted from our sessions.

It can be normal for us to think things through systematically to the nth degree, such as a relationship problem or a decision that needs to be made about the future, which can lead us to become wrapped up in mental knots. However, reason and logic often can't provide the answers we need. I have found myself ensnared in these thinking loops where I dissect the problem and then attempt to piece things back together in a logical, progressive manner to form a convincing argument, but unfortunately, I'm left with even more uncertainty. Betty Edwards, in 'Drawing on the Right Side of the Brain', suggests that the process of art, which engages the right side of the brain, can miraculously unveil solutions that the left brain simply can't reach, as my client discovered with her ball of wool mind. Sometimes, we may want to doodle our problem or seek an image or symbol that represents our feelings or what we hope to experience, and this can guide us in finding the answers we seek.

Symbol and metaphor took on a crucial role when my husband underwent treatment for a year back in 2012. As I trained for the London Marathon, the finish line at the end of the 26.2 miles symbolised for me an end to the challenge. This became a symbol of hope that there would also be an end to the physical trials my husband faced and the personal emotional trials I encountered during 2012 to 2013. I kept the finish line in my mind before, during, and after the actual run as an embodied experience of all things passing, reminding myself that the intensity of the everyday challenges James and I faced would eventually come to an end. The finish line as a symbol was summed up in the ancient and popular wisdom, this too shall pass.

God speaks to us through symbols and metaphors constantly. The whole of creation communicates aspects of God's character, "His Divine power and eternal nature," as explained in Romans 1. This has been my personal experience for a long time. I often pause during dog walks or step outside into the garden to be still, silent and attuned to nature. At times, the warmth of sunlight offers me a sense of God's comfort, while at other moments, simply standing or walking on the ground serves as a comforting metaphor that the Divine Being is the foundation of my existence, supporting me from beneath. The sharp, cold wind during a blustery walk invigorates my senses and reminds me that I am filled with vitality, with the Presence of the Divine continually surrounding and energising me into action.

To experience life more holistically and find greater peace and fulfilment, we need to open ourselves to the treasures of wisdom and knowledge found in the symbols and metaphors that surround us.

Practice

Perhaps you can go and take a look at a nearby tree, or if not, bring one to mind, as trees are such wonderful symbols that offer lessons.

As you hold the tree, or trees in your attention, ask yourself, what might trees tell me about how to live well?

You might notice aspects of the tree that are strong, peaceful or flourishing. Or how trees are true to their own kind, growing according to their own unique template. How trees have a magnificence or a beauty or intrigue. How trees play a vital role in our ecosystem and in cleaning the air.

How do trees speak to you specifically right now, imparting insight and wisdom that you might need to profit from?

Story

By embracing a more holistic perspective through our intuition, somatic awareness and spiritual senses, we can connect with symbols and stories to foster a wider way of knowing.

Stories are an important aspect of self-understanding and communication in all parts of the world. But stories are not necessarily a more primitive way of communication than intellectual explanation and argument. Stories can increase our self-understanding.

Stories help us to know what is meaningful to us. Stories open up profound insights for living more fully. So often, we evaluate ourselves and others as a collection of facts and achievements. However, we are a dynamic story in progress and can enhance our self-understanding through our narrative. We are a living story, and our tale isn't finished until our life is. We can engage with our own story, altering the script if we choose.

In the psychotherapeutic world, Jungian and Transactional Analysts encourage their clients to reflect on fairy tales and films that hold particular significance for them. I recently participated in this exercise and selected The Little Match Girl, The Little Mermaid (both classic fairy tales) and The Painted Veil (a more recent film). These stories have deeply affected me; the first two resonate with a feeling of being hidden and unimportant that the heroines experience. The film provides a sense of restoration and meaning that reflects similar longings in my own life.

Each of us has a story, and we are also the playwright of our own script. In fact, Eric Berne, who created Transactional Analysis in the 1950s, recognized the reality and potency of stories and scripts in an individual's life, which led to the development of Script Theory. This theory describes how we all create a Script from childhood, serving as our way of making sense of the world and our identity. However, we don't just create a meaningful Script; we also act it out, subconsciously playing parts we have written for ourselves, even if we don't enjoy those roles. We might have scripted ourselves as victims of life's circumstances or as neglected individuals, or perhaps we see ourselves as competent overcomers or rescuers who help everyone else, or as loners that others hesitate to approach, or as seductresses who wield power over others. When framed in these terms, it may sound crude, and you might baulk at the idea of having a Script and having typecast yourself. Yet, your Script is an unconscious paradigm, an amalgamation of your beliefs and experiences about yourself, others and the world and how you have made sense of it all.

Are you aware of your own Script and the role that you as protagonist play in it?

For years, my role was to be the good one, the capable one and the self-sufficient one who simply got on with life alone. It became a self-fulfilling experience where I would hide behind others (my naughty siblings, my popular and public husband, the needs of my four children and eventually my health-challenged husband) and embody the role of the good, strong and independent woman, something that society seemed to affirm. After playing this role for many years, unease started to manifest about being hidden, about constantly striving, yet still feeling unworthy and unrecognised. My Script needed some rewriting. Through prayer, insight and good therapy, I have been reframing my self-understanding to something different. I have realised that I have vulnerabilities and needs and that I can reach out to loved ones for support. I also recognise that I am good enough, that my achievements are good enough and that I don't have to follow the old Script that says, do more and be more to have value. I am okay and worthy of just being me. My life feels far richer these days with wonderful deep relationships, less self-condemnation and endless striving, where I can truly value myself and what I do as good.

Your life is a story in progress that follows a subconscious Script. When you are unaware of this Script, you may be mindlessly guided by beliefs that no longer serve you well. It may be beneficial to increase your awareness of your Script and its impact on your daily experiences. Recognising our story and Script allows us to make necessary changes, opening up the possibility of a more complete and fulfilling life.

———⊷⊷———

Practice

What classical/contemporary story has captured your attention?

Which character or theme has especially resonated with you?

How might this reveal elements of your own Script and your role in it?

You can begin to contemplate how you might want to edit your life Script to update it and enable greater flourishing.

Perhaps there is a new role or new story that you want to rescript for your life.

Lessons from Life

When my son was revising for his GCSEs, he quoted from the source of all wisdom, TikTok, "At school, we have lessons in order to pass the test. In life, we have a test to learn our lessons," to challenge why he needed to learn so many irrelevant things. It isn't just the tests that help us learn our lessons, as though life were only ever challenging; everything that happens in our everyday lives is a lesson that enables us to grow in wisdom.

An experience of wholeness is about knowing with our intuition, our bodies and our souls and using symbols, stories and situations. Our everyday situations offer rich and helpful lessons for life.

Another lesson I learnt from running the London Marathon was about my body, that I could endure and overcome more challenges than I ever believed possible. Despite being a jogger since my teens, I typically ran for only 30 minutes at a time. I had never considered or wanted to run a marathon, and it felt unattainable. I decided to run a marathon the moment I left James in the operating theatre for his first surgery and would say it was a God thing because the idea to run a marathon came to me at that moment, and surprisingly, a place was available and it was a rich if very challenging experience.

My realisation grew throughout my training that I could actually do far more than I had ever imagined. This somatic symbolism translated into resilience during my husband's health struggles, as well as the job, housing and financial uncertainties I faced. The medical and practical challenges kept coming for a whole year, but I recognised that there was a finish line and that if I could keep going, I would eventually cross it. My running served as a direct lesson that I could achieve what initially felt impossible and that I needed to trust in my ability to endure and complete the path laid out for me, facing the practical and emotional challenges of 2012 to 2013 which were symbolised in the marathon. The entire training process and the actual run were profoundly impactful for me, feeling like a Divine gift that continues to inspire me.

How things are in one situation can also apply to another, and this is how we learn valuable lessons from life. We can map experiences from one domain to another, uncovering deeper wisdom from everyday occurrences.

Jesus does this frequently in his teachings; he uses everyday examples from life to convey wise lessons. For instance, he tells his listeners that if they know how to give good gifts to their children, how much more does the Heavenly Father know how to give good gifts to His children, using the symbol of family? He also employs the laws of nature to explain that just as a small amount of yeast spreads throughout an entire loaf, in the same way, corruption or goodness can permeate a whole person or community. Additionally, he teaches us that just as we need physical food for our physical appetite, we also require spiritual food to satisfy our spiritual needs.

Lessons for life can be drawn from nature, science, relational patterns, from stories, symbols and everything else occurring in our everyday lives. These offer clues on how we can live more fully in peace and fulfilment in the life we are already experiencing.

———— ❀ ————

Practice

Settle yourself with awareness of your body and awareness of your breath.

Contemplate one or two of the biggest times of learning in your past.

Is there a part of your current life that is significant either due to its beauty or its challenges, which could serve as a lesson of deeper wisdom?

Experiencing Meaning

All knowledge ultimately serves to impart a rich meaning that provides us with a sense of peace and flourishing in our everyday lives.

As a theology student, I used to enjoy exploring the meaning of life with friends, where we would debate what made the most sense philosophically, using developed rationale and overly complex arguments. While these feats of mental gymnastics can be fun, I have discovered a new way to answer the question, what is the meaning of life? The answer actually lies hidden within the question and within ourselves. The meaning of life is the meaning in your life. It is our task to explore the riches of meaning hidden in the life we are already living, using holistic ways of knowing. There are many ways in which we find meaning, and I suggest that the entirety of life offers up moments of meaning, which can even be instances of 'everyday mysticism,' where we sense the reality of the Divine Presence, giving our lives existential and transcendent meaning.

Where do you find meaning in your everyday experiences? Perhaps it lies in seeking peace during a lovely weekend walk, excitement in a holiday you've booked, or connection when meeting up with friends after work. We are all meaning-seeking beings, and we know how to discover it in one way or another. Sometimes, we find meaning through sustainable, healthy and considerate methods. At other times, we may seek meaning in unhealthy and unhelpful ways, such as asserting ourselves boastfully or finding a high through binge drinking. Nonetheless, whether through good means or bad, we constantly seek to experience meaning in our everyday lives.

Psychologists have differed in their description of ultimate motivations as a way for people to find meaning. Sigmund Freud claimed we had a will to pleasure, whilst Alfred Adler posited a will to power. However, my favourite is Viktor Frankl, the existential psychotherapist and Holocaust survivor, who speaks directly about the will to meaning as a foremost priority. He proposed that this will to meaning is greater than the will to survive. He witnessed this firsthand in four concentration camps, and as a psychiatrist, he observed that those of his fellow Jews, who found some meaning beyond mere survival, were better able to endure the horrific torture of the camps.

Experiencing meaning in our lives is vital.

It is not as hard as we think to find meaning in life. It is about living fully in the life you are already living: to observe where you are already finding meaning, the good things and then to focus more of your attention here. If you find it fun and enriching to meet with particular friends, then maybe engage in this with them a bit more seriously, dedicating additional time, awareness and gratitude to those moments. If you find solace in nature, devote more time and attention to that experience. If your passion lies in a project-like writing a book, painting a house, or cultivating a garden—invest more time and attention there. Ultimately, the quality of our awareness and attention will contribute more to our experience of meaning than simply having extra time.

I recently went to visit my adult son who is working abroad in supposedly sunny climes. He'd booked a couple of wonderful places up in the hills and by the coast. But it rained almost constantly. We were unable to walk in the hills, and our swims in the sea were largely in choppy, churned-up brown waters with the wind howling around us. We spent more time under a roof than under sunny blue skies and played more cards than ever. It could've been written off as a disastrous holiday, a disappointment and a waste of money. However, I reminded myself that I was with my precious son (and a daughter, too) and this was where the meaning really lay for me in those six days, more than sunny weather. It was in real connection with these two children, having fun and getting to know them more.

Jesus, by teaching about birds and flowers, loaves and lost coins, was guiding his listeners into finding rich meaning in the everyday. He referred to this as an experience of the Kingdom of God. The Kingdom of God is where we experience the richness of life with the presence of the Divine, which is an experience of wholeness, regardless of our circumstances. This experience of the Divine, which is a meaningful and rich experience of life, is something we find within ourselves and the inscape of life.

Instead of avoiding the question of meaning in life, holistic understanding that enables us to survive and thrive encourages us to courageously and thoughtfully seek the meaning that is already concealed in the everyday. We need to open our eyes, listen attentively, intuit and perceive with our bodies, through everyday lessons and symbols, the presence of beauty, goodness and truth that serve as hidden treasures in the inscape of life.

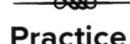

Practice

Settle yourself by bringing your awareness to your breath.

Reflect on the last 24 hours and ponder the moments of meaning that you experienced. It might be in the really small and hidden experiences of the smile of a stranger or the sound of birdsong when you awoke.

Maybe you even sensed something of the Divine coming through to you in those meaningful moments.

Try to account for several moments of meaning and as you recall them, savour them and give thanks for them.

Practice this each day, maybe using bedtime as a way of reviewing your day for meaningful moments.

Chapter 4

Everyday Graces

Do you ever have moments when you're struck by the thought, here I am again? I often experience this in the bathroom at the end of the day while brushing my teeth, feeling that sense of another day completed. The cyclical nature of time, with days, hours and minutes repeating, can highlight the mundane everyday aspect of my existence. The everyday life of brushing teeth, dressing young children, boarding busy commuter trains and sitting at the same desk are our ongoing realities. I recall a cold, grey morning in February when I had three young children at home. Whilst I loved them dearly, the bare trees and milky sky impressed upon me the monotony of the childcare routine of eat, sleep, childcare, repeat. We can all fall into monotonous and mindless rhythms. What is your eat, sleep, X, repeat routine?

Sometimes, the everyday can feel demanding and dreary, making it hard to distinguish one day from the next, leaving us feeling bored or tired. However, hidden within our everyday experiences are graces—moments of meaning where we find peace and fulfilment. We need to become more aware of them, open ourselves up to their existence and embrace the graces in the mundane.

Rahner's 'everyday mysticism' describes moments when a deeper meaning or Divine Presence becomes apparent to us. Perhaps we have slowed down or engaged in some silent contemplation, allowing us to perceive the depth within a situation, a person or ourselves. Paul D'Arcy, a contemporary theologian, builds on this idea using a beautiful aphorism that "God comes to us disguised as our life." What if the very humdrum aspects of everyday life reveal meaning and offer a rich spiritual existence? My own experience suggests that this is indeed the case.

The spiritual tradition I have explored and committed to, Christianity, provides a template for finding meaning and God in very earthy and everyday ways, as demonstrated by the teachings and actions of Jesus. Soaring Gothic buildings and eloquent liturgies are not part of the original landscape of this tradition, so I suggest we turn to the source to rediscover the everydayness of this spirituality. Personally, it reassures me that Jesus had to eat, sleep and excrete—on repeat—just like us. Yet, in his earthly existence, his divinity was manifested. An earthly baby who had an actual mother, grew up through childhood and adolescence to be a carpenter living in Nazareth who, in time, revealed to people the face of God. As his spiritual ministry progressed, he didn't retreat to the lecture halls and libraries of the day but taught outside in nature. He used bread and fish to illustrate deeper truths of God's care; he spat in the mud to make healing pastes for the blind; he enriched his teachings with everyday elements like bread and yeast, shepherds and sheep, farming and foot washing.

When it comes to everyday matters, women are deeply familiar with the earthy, natural and practical existence we all share. Women have often been assigned daily tasks like cooking, cleaning and caregiving in domestic settings. They have been relegated to ordinary spaces rather than the exclusive ones that men have accessed and managed. After spending years in a traditional role as a stay-at-home mum and as a caregiver for my husband, I have grappled with my everyday life, sometimes yearning for something more intellectual, elevated and exciting. However, I have discovered a profound spirituality that has emerged from daily experience, which feels rich and fulfilling. My life has transformed into a journey along a spiritual path where I've learnt to live more holistically and fully in the life I am already leading. I have realised that ordinary activities such as breathing, moving my body, cooking, tidying and caring for children can be experiences of everyday grace. Brother Lawrence, a seventeenth-century Carmelite monk, explains in his book, 'The Practice of the Presence of God', how we can turn daily work into an offering that makes the ordinary sacred.

A pathway to wholeness engages in our everyday experiences, inviting peace and fulfilment to permeate them.

Breathing

The average human takes over 23,000 breaths per day, a nine-digit number that becomes abstract over an average lifespan. Suffice it to say that being human involves a significant amount of breathing. This act of breathing is simply part of daily life, and something many of us often overlook, trusting that our respiratory system functions as our other biological systems do. However, paying attention to this everyday phenomenon can lead to a greater sense of peace and fulfilment in life.

How we breathe reveals how well or unhealthy we are and how we are can be affected by our breathing.

I've had clients in the therapy room, and I can learn a lot about them by the way they breathe. One client breathed very quietly and shallowly, almost imperceptibly. Over time, my intuition about his breathing was confirmed by his story, revealing that he was living on the surface and was very quiet about his own needs; his presence was almost imperceptible to his family. Another client would take a deep breath and then hold it while talking rapidly, often forgetting to breathe until she gasped for air. Her story unfolded to show that she felt the need to gather her energy to go full speed at life and give as much as she could to others, which ultimately left her feeling exhausted. I worked with both clients on their breathing, and it helped establish a different rhythm in their everyday lives.

The fascinating aspect of breathing is that it is an ever-present, everyday activity that we can harness to enhance our wellbeing and spirituality. It is one of the most remarkable treasures hidden within each of us, and when we become aware of our breath or gently control it, remarkable things can occur.

James Nestor, in his excellent book, 'Breath: The New Science of a Lost Art', reveals a fundamental truth about breathing, "Just noticing your breathing can have a calming effect. By simply becoming aware of the breath, we can shift its cadence and depth, nudging our nervous system toward balance." Just as when we truly listen to a child or a friend in distress, we find that they begin to settle and calm; the same applies when we listen to our own breath. It naturally begins to settle into a more balanced rhythm and the length of each breath increases, leaving us feeling calmer and more energised. When we breathe with ease and depth, our nervous system shifts into its parasympathetic state of rest and renewal.

Our nervous systems are designed to put us into fight or flight mode when faced with a threat or even to freeze, shutting down our awareness in the presence of extreme or persistent challenges. However, its preferred resting state is this calm parasympathetic state, (also known as the ventral vagal state, described by Polyvagal Theory). In our modern world filled with distractions and demands, we often spend too much time in the sympathetic state, which is characterised by activation and alertness. While this is beneficial for situations like job interviews or facing the threat of danger, it is unhealthy for our bodies to remain in this activated state for extended periods. We need to reset our nervous systems to restore them to a place of ease, and simply noticing our breath can positively do this, leaving us feeling more peaceful and energised.

In addition to simply noticing our breath, we can also control it. We can choose to deepen, hold, lengthen, or change its rhythm. When we sigh, we invite our breath to properly exhale, serving as one example of how gently controlling our breath allows our nervous systems to reset to their parasympathetic state. While breath awareness and control may not work for everyone, simply being aware of the breath as a symbol offers a way to experience meaning and grace in everyday life.

The Hebrew word for breath and the word for spirit is the same, indicating how breath serves as a symbol of spiritual existence. "*Ruach*" is used interchangeably in older biblical texts to describe both human and Divine breath, as well as human and Divine spirit. This suggests that there might be something inherently spiritual about breathing. I became aware of the spiritual value of breath when I listened to Rob Bell's video series, 'Nooma', (a phonetic spelling of "*pneuma*," the Greek word for both "breath" and "spirit"). He points out that God breathed His "*ruach*" or "*pneuma*," ("breath-spirit") into the first dusty human to bring it to life. He also suggested that the very name of God, "*Yahweh*", meaning "I Am Who I

Am", resembles the sound of breath. We make a sound like "*Yah*" as we inhale and a sound like "*weh*" as we exhale. This suggests that we might even be breathing the very name of the Divine Being. He suggests we join in a great spiritual symphony as all living, breathing beings on earth continuously breathe the name and essence of God by this somatic act of audible participation. This beautiful idea still delights me.

The breath is significant on many levels, whether it practically induces a calmer nervous system, indicates a spiritual presence, or serves as a spiritual experience. Thus, we can say that the breath holds somatic and spiritual value in helping us become more whole.

―――― ∞ ――――

Practice

Breath awareness and prayer (withdraw from the practice if breath practices are triggering or unhelpful).

Notice your breath as it is without judging or trying to adjust it. Allow your breath to settle into an easy rhythm to avoid getting panicky.

Use the inhale as a way of inviting the Spirit into your being.

Use the exhale as a way of inviting the Spirit to settle within you.

Repeat for as long as you wish, engaging you in a

wordless breath prayer of communion with the Divine Presence.

Moving

"In him, we live and move and have our being", says the Stoic Poet referenced in the Bible (Acts 17).

Whilst the pathway to wholeness invites us to slow down and embrace stillness, this does not negate the need for movement. Movement is a fundamental aspect of living, and although we can navigate our lives with greater internal calm and stillness, we can find meaning and wholeness through the actual physical movements of our bodies.

We are already engaged in so much movement, and all the walking, running, reaching, holding, releasing we do in our daily lives can be experienced as an everyday grace.

Through my own running, I have physically pounded my anxiety and fear out on the paths and roads I have traversed. At other times, running has felt like a celebratory connection with the energy of the natural world that flows in, through and around me. However, there have been instances when I have moved mindlessly, running around like a headless chicken while trying to care for my young family and avoid the grief of losing my husband as I knew him. Eventually, I reached a point where I had to stop the headless chicken running and actual running after being diagnosed with burnout in 2016. I needed to slow down and find more stillness in my life, but I still wanted to move and exercise, just in a different way. I engaged more deeply in the practice of modern postural yoga, which proved to be a truly enriching experience of embodiment. Somatic awareness in slower forms of mindful exercise enables a sense of calm and wellness.

How do you enjoy moving? Is it through walking, going to the gym, practising yoga, doing Pilates or some other form of active movement? Do you recognise that when you move more, you can also feel better in your body and being? Movement is not just about making the body beautiful or becoming fit; it is an essential part of everyday life. Movement is not only vital for our physical health, but the natural world is also full of movement. Everything that has life possesses movement within it. However, this natural movement of all living things embodies peace and vitality that contrasts with the exhausting, effortful extra movements that arise in our fast-paced, modern lives.

Movement that is both peaceful and full of life can be found in running water. There is a gentle stream nearby, which flows beneath a small humped-back bridge I sometimes walk on. The water here is shallow and clear, revealing pebbles and rippling riverweed beneath the surface. The constant yet soothing sound of flowing water, and the rippling light on the surface can often draw me into a state of mesmerism, with minutes passing before I realise the dog has gotten lost. Flowing water is one of nature's movements, illustrating how movement can be alive yet tranquil. Experiencing wholeness in everyday life requires mindful awareness of our own movement so that we might also experience the calm and vitality that it enables.

Posture, as well as movement, fosters a unique experience of the everyday grace of being a living, moving bodily being. For instance, standing taller can boost our confidence, whereas dragging our feet around in a collapsed posture can leave us feeling low. Similarly, opening our chest instead of hunching over and breathing more fully can invite positivity into our lives.

Physical postures and movements can connect us to experiences of grace and to the Divine. Many religious traditions emphasise the importance of postures such as kneeling or lifting the head and hands, as well as movements like approaching the altar or bowing to a religious image, which evokes feelings of delight or reverence. Sadly, I believe, somatic involvement has been lost in the church's spirituality, but we can redeem it. We can use posture to embody a way of praying, such as reaching for God's help in high mountain pose or surrendering to God's love in child's pose. Dancing alone in the kitchen, with no particular style but maximum engagement, has become a more recent hobby that leaves me feeling invigorated as if I'm dancing with the Divine. *"Perichoresis"* is the Greek term understood as the Divine dance of love that God experiences within the three persons of the Trinity.

Mechthild of Magdeburg wrote in the thirteenth century about being caught up in this dance of the Divine, and countless other mystics describe how rhythm and movement enable them to know God intimately.

Moving and posturing ourselves with mindful awareness not only benefits our wellbeing but also enables a richer spirituality.

Practice

Experiment with movement.

Standing, hold out your arms raised up in front of you, parallel with your shoulders. As you inhale, draw your arms back and open your chest. Exhale them back to the front. Repeat this opening and closing motion with the in and out of each breath.

It could be a way of physically, emotionally and spiritually opening up to life and energy and help.

Engaging your intention with this movement could be an invitation to the Divine to be present to you as the help, life and energy you need.

Eating

We need to eat to live, but so many of us live to eat.

I had a difficult relationship with food in my late teens, struggling with mild but persistent eating disorders, which were officially undiagnosed but all-consuming and depleting. The problem with eating disorders is that you can't go cold turkey on this addictive type of behaviour. Eating is a necessity and a feature every day of life. We need to eat to live.

Eating can be an everyday grace not only because food is a source of immediate enjoyment but by how food connects us to the wider world. The practice of eating keeps us connected to the earth, as we humbly depend on it to provide for our needs. Eating also fosters gratitude, as it requires effort to till the earth, do the supermarket shopping, chop the vegetables and cook the meal. We can commune with others in a unique way as we share food together. The humility, gratitude and communion around the provision and enjoyment of food serve as an everyday grace that brings moments of meaning and fulfilment to our lives.

Mindful awareness during eating and drinking fosters a more holistic experience for our souls. When I feel anxious and on edge, I pour myself a cup of tea and savour it slowly with mindfulness. As I hold the warm mug, I am reminded of a comforting presence that is always available to me. Taking small sips of tea allows me to experience, with embodied awareness, that this comfort can be felt inwardly. The warmth and familiar earthy flavour of tea provide more than just sustenance for the body; it nourishes and comforts the soul. We can experiment with mindful drinking to explore how it affects us on emotional and spiritual levels.

Mindful eating can also be a way of experiencing a sense of embodied comfort, satisfaction and revitalisation. The experience of being satisfied gastronomically can help us sense satisfaction at a soul level so that we feel connected, comforted and content more deeply. You can try this by eating some bread, chocolate or anything you'd like. Eat or drink slowly, experiencing the fullness of the tastes and textures as you bite, taste, savour and swallow. Allow the experience to settle and nourish your soul at a deeper level.

Our physical appetites point to our emotional and spiritual ones. Food and drink hold soulful significance. While physical food renews our physical "*bios*" life, we also require spiritual nourishment to experience the greater "*zōē*" life. The Bible is filled with food stories, often illustrating spiritual realities. There is the extraordinary account of God providing a substance resembling bread called "*manna*", which literally means "what is it?" when the Hebrews wandered hungrily in the desert after escaping the enslavement of the Egyptians. Jesus recalls this ancient story and tells his perplexed followers that he is the "bread of heaven," and his first miracle was turning water into wine at a wedding feast. The contemporary Christian ritual of communion is a commemorative meal of bread and wine (albeit a very small one!), indicating that Divine grace is somehow bestowed upon people through eating and drinking.

Eating and drinking more mindfully can open up moments of everyday grace that strengthen and satisfy our whole being.

Practice

Jesus says, "I am the bread of life; whoever comes to me will never go hungry, and whoever believes in me will never be thirsty."

You could slowly eat bread or an equivalent in a mindful way that opens up spiritual awareness:

Firstly, become aware that you are eating bread, by doing it slowly, savouring it before swallowing it slowly.

Notice the pathway it takes down the throat into the stomach.

Be aware of how it feels to have eaten the bread, along with any sense of satisfaction.

Extend this awareness to how Divine words and the Divine Presence are to be experienced in a similar way that leaves you feeling satisfied.

Perhaps you could meditate on these words which offer spiritual bread for the soul, "Taste and see that the Lord is good, blessed is the one who takes refuge in him" (Psalm 34).

Cleansing

I remember a workshop where we were invited to visualise a house filled with familiar everyday rooms. In my imagination, I saw a lively kitchen bustling with cooking and kids, a more formal sitting room and dining room, a cosy TV snug and a study. I imaginatively travelled upstairs, where beautifully lit and tidy bedrooms offered comfy beds, with drapes interspersed among clean and sparkling bathrooms. At that time, we were living in school-provided accommodation, and the bathrooms were over thirty years old. So, when the Spiritual Director asked us which room we wanted to be in, I immediately felt drawn to a lovely bathroom in my imaginary house. We were then invited to explore the spiritual significance of this room. I visualised washing away my own dirt and the dirt I had gathered from living in a broken world, feeling a sense of renewal in my soul from this exercise of spiritual cleansing.

Just as regular washing cleans our bodies, so our inner being needs regular cleansing too. This is something that is done to us or for us and requires cleaning materials as it were. The Bible talks about forgiveness as a primary way that people are cleansed, although there is also teaching on how we can be set free from anything that entangles us. So not all dirt derives from our own errors, but sometimes we need freeing from the afflictions and judgments that are done unto us.

When we are forgiven and cleansed, it is not about experiencing judgment and shame for being dirty and sinful, but about experiencing being made clean and whole. We may need to recognise our own brokenness or the pain inflicted upon us, and "*metanoia*", the Greek word for repentance—is the first step. "*Metanoia*" literally means "a transformative shift in consciousness beyond current awareness", and "repentance" is shorthand; repentance invites the Divine outpouring of spiritual cleansing and healing. It involves the removal of brokenness so that our wounds can be healed and our entire being restored to health and wholeness, or, to use another religious term, holiness. To experience wholeness and holiness, which Divine cleansing enables, is much more appealing, I suggest when we consider it this way.

To feel clean is to feel refreshed and ready for life. This process of spiritual cleansing can happen in more designated times of prayer, communion and the Catholic tradition of confession, but it can also happen moment by moment. I remember sitting in the garden last year indulging in my own pity party, when I sensed the Spirit whisper within my being, why don't you release these feelings of self-pity to me? My pity party was anything but fun and this call came as a relief, without judgment, so I did just that and felt instantly freer. The realisation and then relief of not needing to hold on to these gnawing and negative feelings can bring peace and a sense of flourishing.

When we are cleansed by the Presence of the Divine, we get healed and made whole or holy. We feel good, and life feels richer and more enjoyable. Instead of experiencing shame at the dirt and brokenness we hold within, we can simply acknowledge and turn towards Divine allowing the gift of cleansing to bless us.

———— ⚭ ————
Practice

Sense above you a gentle waterfall that pours over, around and through you.

This flow of love can cleanse the life-defying things within you.

Invite the cleansing Presence of the Divine to flow in through you.

As it flows through your mind, allow any dark, depressing and destructive thoughts to be washed out of your mind.

As it flows through your heart space, allow any feelings of darkness, hostility, fear and anxiety to clear out of your heart.

Allow this continual waterfall to be the Presence of Divine Love flowing through you to restore and renew.

Invite and allow this flow of love and renewal into your whole body and being.

Clothing

Back in the 1990s, I worked in Public Relations and Marketing, and I felt I had to look the part. Except I really didn't. I was going through a frugal phase, and shopping, fashion and clothes didn't interest me at all. So, I thought a raid on my mother's wardrobe would provide the clothes I needed for work and I took her 80s shoulder-padded jackets with big shiny buttons, thinking they would be ideal. Whilst this look might even be fashionable for some in today's world I look back at what I wore and cringe at how my clothing missed the mark.

These days, I am more aware of clothing as I've realised it is an expression of self to others and also communicates wellbeing to ourselves. In January, when the weather is cold, I wear my winter uniform of comfy trousers, a favourite wool jumper and cosy boots. Winter clothes have become, for me, something of an emotional blanket against the cold, bare grey of winter. In contrast, the warmer summer months invite flowing skirts, shorts and floaty tops, making me feel adorned by the breezy freedom of summer. Sometimes, it's fun to dress up for an occasion and put on some slap and some shiny jewellery which can make me feel good. But I'll happily wear my sloppy clothes most of the time, to help me feel relaxed and at ease.

Can you notice how certain clothes you wear incite certain feelings? How wearing a bright or patterned garment can make you feel a little more noticeable or energised. Or perhaps you wear that familiar old jumper that is reassuring. Perhaps your work clothes are chosen to tell others that you mean business and that you are to be taken seriously or your social outfits signal to others that you are fun, serious or sophisticated.

Clothes send signals to ourselves about the values

we want to experience and to others the values we wish to convey. The ancient story of Adam and Eve tells of how humanity required clothes from the moment they realised they were naked and vulnerable and so clothing has spiritual significance and can convey everyday grace to us. There are teachings that invite the Spiritual follower to clothe themselves with compassion, kindness, humility, gentleness and patience and to put on love, the new self or Christ. I suggest that to experience greater wholeness, we might sometimes enclothe ourselves with qualities we do not naturally possess. If we feel glum from the winter blues, we could put on the garment of praise that Isaiah proposes, choosing to adopt an attitude of gratitude for Divine blessings. Alternatively, we can place a crown of beauty upon our heads to remind ourselves that we are both beautiful and loved by our Creator.

The practice of wearing clothes can become an everyday grace where we use our imaginative capabilities to also clothe ourselves with Divinely originating qualities that engender wholeness, peace and fulfilment in our lives.

Practice

Where do you feel vulnerable, uncomfortable or upset right now?

Maybe you have feelings of depression, anxiety or anger. Or do you feel empty, exhausted or insecure?

What is the opposite value that you might need right now? Is peace, compassion, confidence, love, energy or hope to name several?

Close your eyes and imagine a beautiful robe or enveloping cloak made of that very quality.

As your imaginative senses feel what it is like to somatically be enclothed, allow your soul to feel what it is like to wear it.

Chapter 5

Sacred Bodies

"The soul that remains attached to bodily concerns is hindered from ascending to the Divine. The female principle...remains close to the material realm." This is the view of Proclus, a Neoplatonic philosopher and Christian thinker and encapsulates antiquity's perspective on women, bodies and matter. Physical matter, including the human body, sat on the bottom rungs of the hierarchical ladder of ascent in Greek thought. Women's bodies—which had more orifices and were seen as open, unfinished and messy—were considered inferior to men's bodies which, by contrast, were viewed as contained, finished and perfect. The objective, in ancient philosophical terms, was to ascend to a disembodied Divine state and bodies, especially women's bodies, were perceived as problematic in this pursuit.

Throughout the centuries, the female body has been vilified as well as objectified, which has made women very aware of their own bodies. In addition, women possess a deep awareness of their unique bodily needs as they manage menstrual issues and potential birthing and lactating functions of their bodies. Moreover, they have a keen awareness of all human bodily needs, having historically been tasked with the care of others. The responsibilities of feeding, cleaning and caring for infants, along with tending to the elderly or sick, have often fallen to women. They are particularly familiar with the nakedness and demands that all human bodies present. Bodies and especially women's bodies have been disparagingly regarded as a problem, or a temptation or irrelevant throughout Western history.

Christian thinkers embraced the early philosophical movement, often mistrusting and dismissing the body in favour of what they considered higher spiritual pursuits. As a result, Christian spirituality became increasingly disembodied, and together with Greek ideals, these influences have permeated centuries of thought, diminishing the importance of our physical existence. This trend was further fuelled during the Enlightenment by Descartes' notion that the mind is preeminent and the body is separate. In our current era, despite all its advancements, a disembodied state of existence is encouraged where we prioritise our minds to engage with intellectual and tech-based ways of knowing and we outsource manual jobs to machinery. We are disconnected more than ever from our bodies and no wonder there is a mental health crisis. We need to reclaim the body.

When we explore the foundational narratives in Christianity, we discover the profound significance of bodies. A unique belief within this tradition is the incarnation, meaning God in the flesh. The God who created humanity became fully and physically human. Jesus lived a fully physical life and did not reject his body at death; rather, it was physically resurrected and ascended into a heavenly existence. This stands as a direct challenge to the dominant philosophies of the time, which dismissed the material world. Throughout his life, Jesus healed countless individuals. He also validated women's bodies by showing compassion to naked and bleeding women who were stigmatised in his culture. The notion that our bodies are inherently unwholesome and unholy represents a corrupt narrative that contradicts the teachings of Jesus. Our physical selves, much like our minds and hearts, can give rise to brokenness and impurity, but they are crafted by the Creator to be holy and whole.

Our bodies are sacred and important, and living a more embodied life can lead to us feeling healthier and more whole. Recent scientific research and secular wellbeing approaches also recognise the significance of the body in books like 'The Body Keeps the Score', by Bessel Van Der Kolk, which explains how stress and trauma are stored in the body. He also emphasises the importance of somatic awareness and its role in healing. Our bodies are innately connected to our minds, hearts and souls, so when one part of us is affected, the whole of us is affected. When we reconnect with our bodies, we can reconnect with ourselves, discover the wisdom of the body that has an innate healing quality, and live a more flourishing life.

We need to reclaim the body as something special and important, as an essential part of our human existence that has been given to us and is valued by the Creator. By living a more embodied life, we find a pathway to health and wholeness, reconnect to ourselves, the world around us, and the Divine and know peace and fulfilment in the whole of our being.

Embodiment

I remember the Christmas just after James came out of the hospital in 2012, during the school holidays: nativity plays and carol services completed, stockings prepared for four kids and then it was Christmas Eve, with eight of us gathered for dinner the next day. I found myself in the supermarket buying readymade everything as I was stressed and shattered. As I pushed the cart, I suddenly realised I was leaning heavily on the handrail, silently hoping it would keep me from collapsing. Overwhelmed and disconnected, I hadn't acknowledged the exhaustion my body was trying to tell me about. I needed to pause, breathe and reconnect with myself before proceeding.

When we live in the body, we have to live in the present moment, as our body can't live in the past or the future. As we experience our physical presence, we, therefore, stay present to what is actually going on in the here and now.

There are several benefits to living a more embodied life. Firstly, we feel more intra-personally connected (with self); feeling disembodied is the norm for many of us where we live in our minds, constantly stuffing them with information, analysis and processing, leading to disconnection from our physical selves. In times of high stress or trauma, we may dissociate, neglecting our bodies altogether. This disconnection or even dissociation can create significant challenges, keeping us entrenched in stress and trauma. It's crucial to reconnect with our bodies if we can.

Secondly, living a more embodied life enhances our interpersonal connections (with each other). In conversations, how often do you catch yourself formulating your next response while the other person is speaking, lost in your thoughts? By fostering somatic awareness, we become more attuned to others, enriching our relationships with vibrancy and fulfilment. During difficult parenting moments, I've noticed that somatic awareness helps me remain present, respond thoughtfully and react less impulsively.

Being aware of our physicality helps us be more attentive, sensitive and connected to ourselves and others. I suggest the same applies to our relationship with the Creator, where being more embodied allows us to actually experience the Divine rather than merely entertain interesting thoughts about Him. "The present moment is the only place where we can truly experience God," explains Shaun Lambert, the Christian mindfulness teacher. My favourite somatic and spiritual practice is sitting cross-legged in my egg chair. As the chair supports my body and I feel the air around me and hear the birds, I become somatically aware. This awareness of myself enables me to bring my authentic self to the Divine and experience Him, rather than a version of myself who is thinking the right things about Him.

How can we better connect with our bodies? I believe mindful awareness offers the solution. Helen Langer, a leading American researcher in mindfulness, states that it is a universal capacity available to everyone. Mindfulness is not just an alternative or extra function that some people access, it is a God-given gift for us all. By concentrating on our physical selves, we can improve our self-awareness. We might notice how our bodies feel at day's end while relaxing on the sofa, evaluate our posture, or observe our breathing and muscle tension in times of stress. We can identify the sensations and tensions within our bodies, as well as the moments when we feel relaxed or exude strength and confidence. As we grow more attuned with ourselves and cultivate greater awareness, we will discover a deeper sense of wholeness, peace and fulfilment.

Practice

Body Scan :

Close your eyes and sit comfortably, but sit still without moving your body and without assessing or judging what you notice in your body.

Firstly, bring your awareness to your feet and any sensations you notice.

Slowly move this awareness up from your feet through your legs.

When you reach your core, notice the softness of the tummy, the movement of the chest and any tension you might hold in your back or shoulders.

Just notice without moving and without judgirg.

Bring your awareness to your arms and hands, before bringing it back up to your neck and finally the head and face.

Do this exercise without moving your body at all and without judging whatever you find. Just notice what sensations are present.

This practice can take 2 minutes or 20 minutes, but notice how you feel at the end.

Physical Senses

Our five physical senses enable us to perceive the world around us and truly connect to it, helpinc us to realise our embodied existence. The senses allow us to take the world inside of ourselves, which is a bizarre, fun and true way of understanding the process which Peter Leithart points out in his fascinating book, 'Traces of the Trinity'. Images enter the pupils, sounds penetrate the ear canals, flavours are taken inside the mouth, smells end up inside the nasal cavity and these physical perceptions travel through our nerves and neurons to our brain, which makes sense of what is around us. We are already integrally and essentially connected to the world around us, but are we always living in the awareness of this somatic connection?

We often take our senses for granted, using them mindlessly or even ignoring them at times. For instance, we might indulge our sense of taste with chocolate after dinner yet remain oblivious to the toast we consume at breakfast. We spend money and time on costly perfumes but overlook the natural scents encountered in nature. While we focus heavily on sight, absorbing countless words and images from our screens, we may miss the stunning morning sky and the fresh leaves unfolding outside our windows. Similarly, we might invest in massages, but overlook the refreshing sensation of water cascading over our skin during morning showers. We tend to believe that listening to our favourite songs will elevate our mood more than the easily accessible sound of birds singing. As my dad would put it, we're missing a trick as we ignore the ready available moments of meaning assimilated through our physical senses.

I recall multiple occasions where I got all four kids dressed, fed and ready for school with a swift bye darling, only to leave and realise I hadn't made eye contact with any of them. This saddened me, prompting the realisation that I needed to slow down and truly see and listen to my beloved children to appreciate them fully. While our senses guide us in a practical way, they also enhance our enjoyment of life. The senses enable life to be a more connecting and fulfilling experience.

What is the most stunning place you've ever visited? A palace, a beach, a forest, a lake or a breathtaking view? When I was 16, my parents took us on a once-in-a-lifetime trip. One day, we ventured on an excursion to some islands. We spent the afternoon on a beach that looked like the one in Leonardo DiCaprio's film, 'The Beach'. It was a gorgeous location with crystal-clear blue water, powdery sand and palm trees swaying in the gentle breeze. I floated in the warm water for what felt like an eternity, experiencing the beach in every captivating way possible. It was a truly special experience with an almost mystical quality, transformed by my physical senses. Engaging our senses with mindful awareness allows life to reveal richer hues, tones and depths.

The senses have a sacred dimension to them too. I love the explanation theologian Elizabeth Moltmann-Wendel gives, "With our senses, we can also experience another dimension of God. Not the God whom many people have learnt in Christianity, the judge, master, ruler, the God from whom we remain eternally distant, but the God who is in all things. By again feeling the breath of creation with our many senses, we find that this God again comes near to us in this breath of creation." Somatic awareness using the five physical senses enables the world around us to become more alive. In this way, we can experience the Divine in a more visceral, sensory and experiential way.

But we need to slow down and notice the every day, employing our physical senses to really appreciate the hidden treasure. We need to truly savour the world with our senses of sight, smell, sound, taste and touch so we have more peace and can live more richly and fully.

Practice

Sit comfortably and notice how your body feels and how your breath is.

Then slowly and mindfully, wherever you are, find:

Five things to look at (just choose certain objects, people and things around you).

Four things you can hear (from the louder noises to distant and nearer ones).

Three things you can touch (clothes, jewellery, fabrics and bricks).

Two things you can smell (you can smell part of yourself or your clothes).

One thing you can taste (what lingering taste is in your mouth).

Are you able to extend your awareness beyond the physical senses to how the Divine might be present through these experiences?

Our physical senses might give us a sense of beauty, peace, hope, comfort and energy that help us sense God's presence or character to us through these experiences.

Inner Sensing

When we focus our attention on what is happening within the body, we discover a fascinating physical landscape within ourselves.

Eugene Gendlin, a philosopher and psychotherapist, introduced a technique known as focusing in the late twentieth century. He observed that individuals with a stronger felt sense of their bodies were more capable of change and healing. Gendlin realised that each person's inscape possesses a unique somatic configuration and that exploring our internal bodily experiences naturally guides us toward healing. It is well understood that the body carries emotional pain and just like it works to heal from cuts, bruises and illnesses, it also strives for healing and wholeness in response to emotional distress. Similar to how we allow ourselves the time and space needed to recover from a physical injury or illness, we can also afford time and space to the felt sense of psychological pain, allowing the body's wisdom to process and heal emotional suffering.

I worked with a client named Mike, who noticed a persistent sensation in his chest, describing his felt sense as a ball of butterflies. Over several weeks, as he allowed this feeling to surface, he identified it as anger he had suppressed for 40 years. Mike had faced significant emotional neglect and harshness from his single mother during childhood, never standing up to her verbal attacks. As he connected with this heavy sensation, his anger began to emerge, which he shared with me. After a few weeks of expressing and processing the pain and anger from his traumatic past, he reported a resurgence in his creativity and was able to return to songwriting. Many people bury painful emotions, leading them to reside deep within our physical selves. This repression can eventually result in depression. By creating space to confront these trapped feelings, we can unlock the psychosomatic systems, allowing for emotional processing and fostering greater healing and wholeness.

There is a difficult-to-say biblical Greek word, "*splagchnízomai*", which translates to "moved by compassion" and refers to the inner organs or gut, which the ancients believed was the source of profound emotions. It was frequently used to describe Jesus' deep compassion and mercy. This reveals that the Divine-human experienced life with an embodied awareness, guided by his inner sensing to heal and forgive those in need. A whole way of living invites us to engage in embodied listening to our felt sense, promoting deeper healing and wholeness.

Practice

A Brief Focusing Exercise

Clear the space by sitting quietly and still, settling your body and breath.

Allow a bodily sensation to emerge into your awareness without judging it. It might be a felt sense of tightness, heaviness, emptiness, constriction, a ball, a block or a band in your stomach, heart space, chest, head or throat.

Perhaps there is a word, a phrase or even an image that captures the essence of this felt sense or you can use the words just suggested to describe the felt sense.

Ask the felt sense what it is trying to communicate.

Accept whatever comes to you without judging.

Hold this felt sense in the body in your awareness, maybe bringing your breath to this physical part of your body. Take your time.

Notice if anything changes.

Be aware of how you feel somatically and emotionally at the end of this focusing exercise.

Posturing

How we posture ourselves can make all the difference.

I was recently surprised by my supervisor's advice when I shared how a client, Dean, felt down all the time. My supervisor simply responded, "Well, tell him to put a pencil in his mouth so it can't droop, and to look up rather than down!" She had extensive experience working in prisons and had numerous physical interventions for depression, anxiety and anger. While I questioned whether it was as straightforward as she suggested, there was indeed some truth in her advice for him.

Have you ever taken the time to observe your own physical posture? Do you slump your shoulders, push your head forward, inflate your chest or dump your weight on one side? How about your gait? Do you walk head first, chest first or pelvis first? Do you drag your feet or turn your feet outwards? Do you take large, confident strides or smaller, timid steps? How we stand, walk and even sit is a reflection of how we might be as a person. The history of our experience is held in our body and is manifested in our posture and movements. The growing world of Somatic Therapy is researching and using body awareness to help heal people because it works. By paying attention to our posture, movements, gestures and gait, we can transform these somatic signals into something valuable.

Pat Ogden, a Somatic Psychotherapist, has written

about her own experience in Sensorimotor Psychotherapy. She describes how, as an academic woman existing in a man's world, she always felt she needed to get ahead to be noticed and had to strive to be acknowledged. She relays how her head was always in a forward position, her walking was quick and she primarily resided in the front of her body. Reading her account, I instantly recognised my own posture and gait, as I too tend to live in the front of my body. Following her advice to sense into the back of the body, brought an incredible sense of relief. It felt as though I was finally settling into something I had always yearned for, an everyday gem hidden in my current life. By bringing my awareness to the back of my body, I began to experience a deeper sense of calm and completeness.

This newfound awareness and change in posture led to spiritual growth where I am able to let the Divine support me. As someone who naturally strives for self-sufficiency, I sometimes find it challenging to trust God. However, by tuning into my back body, I can better lean into the Divine and permit myself to be embraced by God. I notice a decrease in my heart rate, a slowing of my voice and a deeper spiritual connection to the One who supports me.

To posture ourselves in peace, strength and flourishing, we have to live in the whole of our body where we aren't collapsing, drooping, lagging behind or striving ahead. Our posture not only echoes the adaptations we've made to cope in a broken world but reinforces that reality. Healing can occur by gently imitating positivity until we truly embody it as we practise living fully in our bodies.

Quite recently my sister pointed out that my shoulders had become noticeably hunched since my husband's hospitalisation due to his strokes and fall. I hadn't realised this until she mentioned it. It dawned on me that I had been holding onto tension and was in a constant fight-or-flight state as my arms and shoulders coiled tightly as if ready to spring into action. I began to apply the fake it till you make it approach by gently and gradually relaxing my shoulders, pulling my shoulder blades back and opening up my chest to adopt a more relaxed posture. Initially, I felt somewhat exposed and couldn't fully change my physical stance, but with continued practice it helped me to become more relaxed overall.

The whole of our being is mirrored in our posture. The way we present ourselves reflects the psychosomatic truths we possess. By making subtle changes to our movements and posture, we can enhance our physical, emotional and spiritual well-being. To achieve wholeness, we must welcome curiosity into our embodied experiences, allowing for a deeper sense of peace and flourishing.

Practice

You might want to look in a mirror at your posture. What does it communicate (to you and to others)? Defended, open, disappointed, confident, inflated, hopeless, indifferent?

You could very slowly and gently change your posture, but be led by the body, not by your mind, engaging a felt sense of how your body might want to move towards a more whole and integrated posture.

You might find yourself extending your spine upwards, lifting your head a little, settling your shoulders down, softening your knees and grounding through your feet.

Play with your posture by seeking to embody certain qualities e.g. confidence, peace, friendliness, strength and so on. Ask your body how it might want to posture itself to adapt to and embody these qualities.

Holy Whole

Wholeness in body, mind, heart and soul is not just about living fully in this life, but also in the eternal realm.

"If we find ourselves with a desire that nothing in this world can satisfy, the most probable explanation is that we were made for another world..."

To what extent do you agree or disagree with author C.S. Lewis's thoughts? Do you hold beliefs in heaven, fate, something, or perhaps nothing at all? Maybe you choose not to ponder these questions and have become adept at dismissing them, or possibly the uncertainty occasionally unsettles you during vulnerable moments. While I firmly believe in an existence beyond this life, as Lewis expressed, I sometimes find myself frustrated with my own faith tradition, which tends to imply that salvation equates to a disembodied, ethereal state, which is presented as a desirable outcome.

We all have beliefs about what lies beyond death; even choosing to disregard this topic is itself a choice. The evidence from our physical instincts, near-death experience accounts, biblical stories and the Divine resurrection offers a strong argument for the continued existence of both our physical and spiritual selves. Every part of our being craves to live fully, healed, healthy and whole. Such complete fulfilment in life is never entirely achieved during our time here. Not only do we yearn for wholeness, but we also abhor death—we desire everlasting life in perfect health. I believe that this kind of eternal wholeness is a rightly ordered longing and is possible beyond the grave.

A bodily, eternal life brings hope. If my life were solely about my present experience, it would be very disappointing. My husband has changed from who he was thirteen years ago. We can no longer participate in the same activities that were once available to us. There is a different level of emotional depth and intimacy in our marriage, now characterised by loss. So much has gone, and there is grief that has had to be processed. Daily life continues to be challenging for James; merely getting dressed, eating and bathing is a struggle. Engaging in any work is exhausting, and participating in regular conversations can be overwhelming. If his current life were all he had, that would be terrible. This is not why we both have faith, but it certainly gives us hope beyond our practical and physical existence.

We both hold hope for something greater: a state of healing, health and wholeness that is holy which is both spiritual and eternal. I often fantasise about meeting him in the heavenly realm with our renewed physical bodies and restored neurological networks for the first time, knowing that we won't even need to say anything. We will both just understand that what was then is no longer, and there will be a profound connection and an overwhelming sense that all is well; simply seeing and holding each other will be enough. I believe that we will both be wholly restored in body, mind and soul and that this is a holy thing, this ultimate wholeness.

Becoming whole means paying attention to the somatic and the spiritual in the here and now. Wholeness invites you to consider and soften to the possibility that your physical body is holy, spiritual and eternal and there is an invitation to be holy whole beyond death.

———

Practice

Ecclesiastes was the first biblical author who really attracted my attention. He grappled with the question of meaning and offered little in terms of answers beyond pointing to an eternal dimension, in these words, "God has set eternity in the human heart."

As you reflect on this notice what comes up for you; hope, irritation, peace, disbelief, longing or anger?

Whatever response arises, without judging it, hold it in your awareness. You might notice how your response manifests in your body, and perhaps offer it to the Divine as a silent prayer of longing or protest.

Chapter 6

Spiritual Earth

Have you ever hugged a tree and asked it to speak to you?

I have! I attended a brief evening retreat a few years ago and after some movement and mindfulness activities, we took a barefoot walk and discovered a tree that seemed to speak to us. We approached this inviting tree and either placed a hand on it or leaned our bodies against it to listen to its message. At first glance, it might sound kooky, and some religious folks might even call it dodgy. However, I was open to the experience, knowing that all of creation conveys the message of the Creator. As I touched the tree, I sensed a quiet invitation to reflect on how its sturdy, upright trunk towered above the other trees, with its foliage reaching for the sky. It conveyed an important lesson, whispering its wisdom to me, seek the light above, and you will flourish. Some may say that it was God communicating through the tree, or that I was simply using the tree metaphorically to gain personal insight, or perhaps that the tree was genuinely talking to me. Personally, I believe it encompasses all of the ideas at work.

We are rightfully worried about environmental sustainability, yet I believe the more significant reasons for preserving our planet are often overlooked. The earth is not merely a resource to manage for future generations; it is also a somatic and spiritual reality of our lives that helps us experience peace, resilience and a sense of true vitality. Much of the overwhelm and dissatisfaction many of us feel stems from our disconnection from our bodies and spiritual selves, but also from nature. Becoming aware of the natural world around us can enhance our sense of wellness and wholeness.

John O'Donohue, the poet, philosopher and priest, expresses that "The body is the clay house of the soul. Walk in nature as if you are remembering who you are," emphasising that nature offers a re-humanising experience. In our fast-paced, fragmented and tech-driven world, we often find ourselves living more virtually than fully. Scientific research supports the notion that nature has healing properties and enhances our wellbeing. Immersion in nature engages our five senses, allowing us to connect with the external world through its sights, sounds, scents and sensations. This heightened somatic awareness cultivates feelings of calm, strength and joy. You might find this through dog walking, gardening, sailing or simply enjoying the stars, a favourite view, or a sunset with your holiday cocktail! There isn't a prescribed way of being in nature, but it is important to experience it somatically in one way or another.

In 2013, as my husband began his recovery, the metaphors and symbols found in the natural world deepened my understanding of my own feelings. The stunning hills surrounding the area where I lived reminded me that a beautiful future existed, even if it was not yet visible to me. The transition from winter to the budding of trees sparked genuine hope within me that life could renew following the losses from my husband James' medical treatments. One day, my friend Alice gifted me a bouquet from her garden, apologising for its bedraggled appearance. After she left and I went to put it in a vase, I discovered a spray of dog roses among the bouquet, complete with thorny stems and delicate petals, yet possessing a remarkable fragrance. In that moment, I asked the Divine, "What message do you have for me in this dog rose?" and I felt a quiet response within me, saying, "Everything I have created holds meaning about me."

I am convinced that nature not only calms our nerves and provides a breathtaking backdrop for our moments of reflection, but it also imparts wisdom about the Divine Being and the deeper purpose of humanity's existence.

Catholic theologian Teillhard de Chardin encapsulates it like this, "The Divine presence is always manifest in the world and in everything that exists. It is in every part of the universe, not as something external, but as its very heart." In his book 'The Open Secret', Anglican theologian Alistair McGrath also describes how nature conveys Divine truths and is openly available to any of us. The Bible itself tells us that "since the creation of the world, God's invisible qualities—His eternal power and Divine nature—have been clearly seen, being understood from what has been made..." Many people will say that their spirituality is connected to nature, and I suggest this is because nature is a very real, physical demonstration of the reality and character of the One who created it.

At every level, nature is essential for life, physically providing resources for our bodies, fostering psychological and emotional regulation for our nervous systems and helping us feel calmer and more connected. Moreover, on a deeper and more meaningful level, nature allows us to establish a connection with the Creator. There is an invitation for those who feel disconnected to engage with creation to foster a spiritual connection with the Divine.

Ground

We are made of the ground and spend all our days upon it. We truly are grounded beings.

I remember the thrill of discovering a somewhat inaccessible beach during a holiday abroad. Using a little motorboat, we dropped anchor a short distance away. As we swam to the beach, we noticed other bathers appearing a very odd colour, with patchy skin as if they were dreadfully ill. Upon landing, we joined the locals in the activity of slathering mud all over our skin, hoping to reap the benefits of rejuvenated skin or at least relief from sunburn. It was a messy affair and a rare opportunity in our lives to get so thoroughly covered in the raw material of the earth.

How connected to the earth do you feel? So often, we are utterly out of touch with the ground, which is why Thich Nhat Hanh, the monk and mindfulness teacher, so eloquently encourages us to "Walk as if you are kissing the earth with your feet."

There is something wonderful about connecting to the earth, whether we are walking or lying on it or smearing ourselves in mud! After all, we are made of the dust of the ground whether we are drawing the reference from religion or science, so we are already part of the ground, an extension, you could say.

As we connect with the ground, so we connect with reality, with our real material embodied selves and with ultimate reality.

Perhaps this is why the philosophers speak of the Ground of Our Being in referencing the transcendent, numinous Other that many call God. We are made of the dust of the earth, and we can perceive our origins in the Creator—the Ground of Our Being—in a similar way. Each of us rises from the ground and eventually returns to in...or to God. Aren't the overlaps subtly and remarkably alike? At times, I find it challenging to settle and relax, allowing the ground to support me. Similarly, I sometimes resist God's love and sovereignty, as I prefer to take charge of my life. I've discovered that by practising awareness of the physical ground, which is always present, dependable and strong enough to support me, I can cultivate trust in the Divine's presence and sustenance. Having this earthly faith does not imply that the ground is God; rather, it serves as a conduit through which we tangibly experience God.

Connecting physically and with all of the senses to the ground is highly beneficial for our wellbeing. This is why the wellness industry promotes grounding techniques and you can even purchase grounding sheets to sleep on, enabling your body to connect with the earth as if you're an electrical device needing earthing, to avoid feeling overwhelmed! When I feel anxious or overly excited, my voice quickens and rises, my heart rate spikes and I often feel detached from those around me, and even from myself. In those moments, I'm not particularly grounded. Perhaps you've experienced this too? A sense of disconnection and remoteness, instead of feeling calm and connected to yourself and others, which we describe as being grounded. Engaging in practices like body scans, breathing exercises and mindfully using our physical senses can effectively ground us in the present moment.

I was on a solo retreat some years ago, reading Barbara Brown Taylor's book, 'An Altar in the World', which remains true to its title and inspires readers to not only believe but also to experience the earth as a spiritual and sacred place. Following her lead, I left my shoes in my hotel bedroom and went for a barefoot walk. It lasted over two hours, so by the end, my sensitive feet were scratched and achy, but the experience was profound. I felt much more connected to the earth, more human and more spiritually connected to the Creator.

The Ground-God holds us. It is the substance from

which we are formed and to which we return. When we connect to the Ground-God through our bodies, something spiritual can also alchemise, where we feel more earthy, more human and somehow more Divine. Living in wholeness is about living in connection with the earth, through our physical bodies that leads to a connection to the spiritual ground of our being.

Practice

Find a time of day when you can practice walking without shoes.

Take off your shoes. Go stand outside if possible.

Feel the texture and solidity of the ground through the soles of your feet.

Then, walk very slowly, feeling the ground through your feet.

Become aware of the physical sensations of heat or cold coming up.

Be aware of the connection you have with the earth.

If it is warm enough outdoors (otherwise indoors) lie down on the ground.

This time, use the whole back of your body to sense the ground beneath you. You automatically trust the ground to hold you each and every moment, but become aware of this trusting attitude. See if you can extend your trust to trusting the Ground of Your

Being to hold you securely, holding you just as you hold many concerns in your heart and soul.

Allow yourself to sink into it, to be held in the Ground of Steadfast Love and Peace.

Water

Without water, there is no life. Water is life-giving whether we are drinking it, washing in it or even having fun in it.

Do you still feel that childhood thrill when you first spot an outdoor swimming pool? Perhaps you're on vacation, and you catch a glimpse of the turquoise water sparkling under the sun and a wave of excitement washes over you. My body has been trained to respond this way since childhood, although now it doesn't always mean I'll jump into a pool or the waves at first sight. However, I recall my friend Mark, a 50-year-old man, arriving at a kid's swimming party to pick up his children. His excitement led him to exclaim, "Excuse me!" as he quickly stripped down to his boxers and dived into the outdoor pool, leaving both kids amused and adults in disbelief!

Many people find being in water appealing. Perhaps bathing in water prompts somatic memories of being in the womb, floating carefree. Or maybe we sense the ancient echo of the primordial soupy waters from which creation originated and the water that is us. There is something life-giving about drinking, being close to or immersed in water.

The human body is also largely composed of water. Fascinatingly, we lose water as we progress from infancy (78% water) to elderhood (45%); as we lose our vitality, we lose water too. Water brings life, and a lack of it leads to decay. Every living thing relies on water, and it is the most valuable resource on our planet. Unfortunately, our Western privilege often causes us to take this bounty for granted. All life around us—plants, animals and even our machines— need water and without it, the world becomes dirty, parched and lifeless.

Water, I suggest, is one way the Divine communicates His presence. We need to have our thirst quenched not only physically but also emotionally, mentally and spiritually. Life can feel so demanding, and our souls can feel so parched that we need inner spiritual refreshing. Water is a beautiful symbol of how the spiritual mechanics of revitalisation may come. Jesus said, "Whoever drinks the water I give them will never thirst. Indeed, the water I give them will become in them a spring of water welling up to eternal life." There is a source of Divine refreshment that leads us into eternity. When people ask me how I have coped in the last 13 years, without a doubt, it is because of the spiritual streams of water I can access.

We have physical hunger and thirst but also spiritual ones and our body-being can communicate to us when things are running dry. There have been many, many times in my life that I've sensed my deep spiritual dryness, and this has led me to reach out to the Water of Life and ask for refreshment. Sometimes, I sense the Divine Presence flowing around me and cleansing me; at other times, I sense the Water of Life gently bathing me. At other times, I sense the vitality of the Divine Presence rising up within me and refreshing me.

Just as you need water in your life for cleansing, bathing, drinking and life around you, the Divine Presence works in the same way. Water, the Water of Life is always present to enable us to find health and wholeness in the everyday.

Practice

Imaginative Meditation

Using any of your physical senses, imagine that you are floating in a river which is safe, beautiful and warm. Your body floats along, held by the water.

You feel the water flowing around you. Feel the sensation of water flowing over your skin as it carries you along.

Allow this flow of water to also permeate the boundary of your body so that the flow of water is also able to flow within you.

As it flows through your head, allow it to cleanse away thought processes that are not life-giving and as it flows through your heart space, carry away those emotions that are not enlivening.

Be open to the flow of the Water of Life that flows around, in and through your whole being.

You can use your intention to imagine the river flowing beyond you and out through situations that need peace and life.

Greenery

During the lockdown, I frequently walked along the outskirts of my village, a route I call The Loop. This 20-minute stroll meanders through fields and trees, passing by a small stream. Although it's too brief for a proper dog walk, it presents a charming pathway filled with diverse sights, sounds and experiences. One particular area features nine trees closely clustered together. These trees are impressively tall, their foliage crowning the uppermost canopy, revealing sturdy, bare trunks that soar skyward. I loved stopping in the centre of this tree circle, where the trunks would often rub against each other in the wind, producing a unique resonant sound. Being enveloped by their majestic presence and the accompanying sound created a truly magical atmosphere.

In the shifting landscape of uncertainty that covid brought to us all, I felt the solidity of the trees whispering, solidity and certainty exist, right here and now. I also noticed the towering heights of these trees and inwardly experienced inspiration, recognising that there are strong and beautiful realities much bigger than myself. It was as though the trees were witnessing that my experience of being locked down was less real than the certainty and beauty they spoke of. This was a profound spiritual experience where I understood that the trees were pointing to the Divine's existence, strength and beauty, which couldn't be overshadowed by lockdowns and limitations.

Trees, plants, flowers, grass and all green life on earth reveal deeper truths. For me, trees hold a special significance; I cherish them, even though I struggle to recall all their names. When life's relentless demands leave me feeling unsettled, taking a moment to observe trees helps me find calm and stability. I see that trees don't strive to grow or root themselves anywhere other than where they naturally are. They don't express dissatisfaction with their shape, height, appearance, or location, nor do they wish to emulate other trees! Each tree is content to be exactly where it is, to be what it is, and to grow in its unique way. This serves as a beautiful metaphor for peace and acceptance, reminding us to be grounded and thriving right where we are and in who we are.

I recommend that we re-evaluate the beauty, richness and resources of nature. It serves not only our physical protection and nourishment but also supports our entire being, including our spirituality. Observing the lilies of the field that thrive effortlessly offers us valuable lessons on flourishing by embracing our true nature.

We need to slow down and rediscover the truth and treasure that is all around us in nature, in the things that grow upon the earth. Perhaps you could walk more mindfully or just stand amongst the trees like you would float in a bath, bathing your senses with the rustling leaves, the dancing leaves and the shifting light rays. Or perhaps you might engage with gardening in a way that is more aware and connects you to nature.

By connecting with nature, we align with our instincts and recall our true selves. Our society often seeks to diminish our humanity, but when we mindfully immerse ourselves in the natural world, we enter a state of wholeness that reestablishes our connection to ourselves, the environment and the Creator.\

Practice

Visualise a beautiful garden. It can be real or imagined or a combination.

Explore the space.

What do you see? Trees with different shades of green leaves, sunlight shining through, colourful flowers, grass, maybe a pond or stream?

What do you hear? Maybe birdsong or you hear a breeze in the trees or the sound of running water.

What do you feel? The warmth of the sun on your skin, bare feet on the ground, a gentle breeze in your hair?

Can you smell the scent of flowers, grass and nature in her beauty?

What does this imaginative scene communicate to you that is positive? Be with that experience and savour it.

Animals

A connection with animals deepens our sense of wholeness.

Are you an animal lover? Enjoying animals comes to us in different ways. During my own childhood, my dog, Crumpet, showered me with unconditional love, sleeping by my bedside until her legs could no longer manage the stairs. More recently, I confess to enjoying social media reels featuring kittens and puppies playing with babies and toddlers to elicit laughter from them which then sets me off. Another recent joy is a stray peacock who regularly visits our garden and seems to regard me as a potential mate, displaying his stunning tail feathers in a magnificent fan.

Animals enhance our lives and contribute to our mental and emotional wellbeing. Our beloved dog, who was professionally trained and then gifted to us for retirement before becoming too lame now visits the wellbeing buses that my husband's charity takes to schools. Pupils find comfort in petting or cuddling him when they're uncertain about tasks or choosing a friend to sit with, and our own children experience emotional comfort in his soft, calm presence too. Pets provide unconditional love and are crucial for alleviating stress and anxiety, as the scientific data backs up. Creatures in the wild also entertain, enliven and enrich our lives and a world without animals would be quiet and desolate.

As we become aware of the diverse animal life surrounding us, we understand that animals serve not just for our entertainment, affection and our wellbeing, but that we humans hold responsibility for their survival and welfare. We care for our pets, cultivate flowers for the bees and protect endangered species, recognising that animals rely on human kindness and consideration for their existence. The animals for which we take responsibility, both directly and indirectly, remind us that we are not the only important beings on this planet, preventing us from falling into unhealthy self-absorption.

The medieval monk Francis of Assisi reminded his audiences that animals are unfragmented beings existing in harmony with themselves and their environment. He suggested that they can guide us toward healthier and holier lifestyles. Unlike humans, animals fully inhabit the present moment and when we engage with them through care and interest, we are brought into that same sense of present wholeness. Francis referred to animals as his brothers and sisters and taught that all creatures are part of the same Divine community, urging individuals to approach animals with kindness and respect.

As we give animals our attention—noticing, enjoying and caring for them—we also enhance our own wellbeing. Instead of merely stroking a pet or giving a fleeting glance at the lambs in spring, perhaps we can slow down to truly appreciate and enjoy the animal kingdom. Animals teach us to embody Divine attributes of gentleness and care and as we engage with them, our experience of their affection and immediacy helps us feel good in the present moment.

Practice

Bring to mind the affection, fun, love or comfort you have gleaned from animals, especially a personal pet if you have ever had one.

Maybe some images or somatic memories emerge. Choose a memory or collective memory that centres around a pet or animals where positive emotions were felt.

Allow the memories to become a felt sense of that animal(s), enjoying the affection, physicality and presence of the animal(s).

How does it leave you feeling now?

Seasons

What season is your favourite?

I cherish autumn, particularly train rides where golden and red leaves sweep by my window. During my university days, I enjoyed cycling among the towers and spires as mist settled like an autumn blanket over the city. Recently, spring has emerged as a powerful symbol of hope for me, bringing new greenery and longer days filled with light. I always welcome summer, and winter has its own serene beauty. Living in the British Isles provides such delightful variety that even with the rain and cold, I would never wish the seasons away.

The seasons are determined by the position of the sun in relation to the earth and each season is characterised by certain weather whether you live in the outer hemispheres or the tropics. If you're British, you'll be culturally conditioned to spend a lot of time observing and commenting on the weather. But how attuned are you to the season of life you are in?

I know I'm reaching the change, as my grandmother would quietly say, a bit embarrassed, as if it was about something obscene! This period of menopause is marked by emotional turmoil and loss: my youth is slipping away, my muscles are weakening, my children are leaving and my heart aches. I'm transitioning from the summer of my life into autumn, beginning to appreciate the beauty and wisdom this season brings as I bask in the final summer rays. Despite the underlying sorrow, I recognise I'm stepping into a new chapter filled with fresh opportunities. But by acknowledging the season we're in, we can become more aware of its impact on us and adjust ourselves to the seasons of life.

Is there a season or a weather system that reflects your current experience?

You might feel as though you're in a wintry phase where loss prevails and nothing seems to thrive. Alternatively, you could be basking in spring-like vitality with new opportunities emerging. Or perhaps you're facing turbulent times, feeling buffeted by relentless winds and rains, struggling to stay upright against the storm. Regardless of your current experience, you are in a particular season; if it's sunny, take pleasure in it and if it resembles a harsh winter, remember that it will eventually pass.

Life isn't merely a straight path; it weaves through peaks and troughs, going in all sorts of different directions. Seasons constantly change in our lives: we experience storms and sunshine, moments of winter and bright sunny days. Throughout this journey, some aspects will fade away while new beginnings will arise. Storms may strike us hard, but gentler days will heal us.

Mary Oliver, in her poem 'Lines Written in the Days of Growing Darkness' reminds us of the messages nature gives us about the whole reality of our life,

"Every year, we have been

witness to it: how the

world descends

into a rich mash, in order that

it may resume."

The seasons teach us how life operates on this earth and inspire us to live in hope as new growth emerges each year. To become more whole, we must fully engage with each season, learning, growing and embracing the goodness found within them.

———— ⁘ ————

Practice

Read these words of Ecclesiastes, which describe the seasons of life as well as their passing, to help you discern what season you are in currently:

There is a time for everything
and a season for every activity under the heavens:

a time to be born and a time to die,

a time to plant and a time to uproot,

a time to kill and a time to heal,

a time to tear down and a time to build,

a time to weep and a time to laugh,

a time to mourn and a time to dance,

a time to scatter stones and a time to gather them,

a time to embrace and a time to refrain from embracing,

a time to search and a time to give up,

a time to keep and a time to throw away,

a time to tear and a time to mend,

a time to be silent and a time to speak,

a time to love and a time to hate,

a time for war and a time for peace.

OLIVIA SHONE

Chapter 7

Transforming Suffering

Parker Palmer, the Quaker thinker, reflects, "Wholeness does not equate to perfection; rather, it involves embracing brokenness as an essential aspect of life." This resonates with the views of many spiritual authors and psychologists alike. Yet, are we truly open to hearing these perspectives? Accepting brokenness and pain can be challenging, leading us to either reject them or desperately seek to repair what's damaged. I've noticed this tendency in my own Christian environment, which often promotes a triumphalist faith that tends to overlook and downplay grief and suffering.

After several years of James' difficulties, I became weary of this bias. It wasn't that I had swapped hope for cynicism, but I longed to hear from those who, like Job in the Bible, had truly faced the confusion and pain that arises from the mystery of suffering. I sought to discover how I could attain the promised peace that passes all understanding amidst the suffering.

I've become more of a Christian Mystic in recent years as there is space for mystery and suffering in this path which is completely at one with the wider faith tradition. Suffering cannot always be resolved, and there is an air of mystery surrounding it. Whether it is the small, subtle sufferings of a friend snubbing you or the profound loss of a child, at some point, on some level, in this life, we will all encounter the mystery of unresolved pain and suffering. We need a way of living that engages with it while allowing for wholeness despite it.

Women are well acquainted with suffering. Whilst all people suffer, the statistics show that women are much more likely to be victims of physical and sexual abuse along with experiencing social oppression more frequently than men. Beyond facing external oppression and hardship, women also confront bodily challenges such as the potential pain of childbirth or miscarriage and the emotional and physical struggle of menopause. Being a woman often means being more acquainted with pain and suffering, and this observation does not lessen the suffering of men; rather, it emphasises the reality that such experiences are largely inevitable for women. Sometimes, we can alleviate suffering, such as when we rescue the abused or assist war-torn communities. Nonetheless, some struggles and suffering are inescapable, making it essential for us to acknowledge and accept them. Accepting suffering can lead to its transformation.

What's troubling you right now? Is it a failing relationship, work stress or lingering sadness? Or perhaps it's the overwhelming sense of fragmentation in today's busy world. Much like the experiences of women, many people's struggles remain concealed and persistent. It's like an immovable object, such as a rock or a fallen tree in the path of a river, disrupting the flow of your daily life that you wish would shift but remains steadfast.

There is a way through suffering, which involves accepting the immovable realities and flowing around them. When we accept and even embrace the reality of suffering, it does not lead us to become overwhelmed, hopeless and defeated; instead, we begin to realise that our actual self is bigger than the suffering. By stepping back and observing our suffering, we understand that we are indeed carrying it and that we are still alive. Slowly, we may find that the presence of suffering transforms. For myself, the mystery of Christ carrying and submitting to his cross, yet rising from the dead, serves as a symbol for embracing and transforming suffering.

The journey to wholeness encourages you to embrace the strength of women and to confront both the visible and hidden pain and suffering in daily life. This acceptance fosters peace, and over time, we might discover new growth in the areas that suffering has created.

Mystery

Some mysteries confound us, whilst others intrigue us.

Crosswords often stress me out. Despite a solid education, when I'm with someone who seeks help doing a crossword, I go blank. Akin to a drunkard I stumble through the empty corners of my mind, unable to find the word to solve the mystery. The repetitive mini-puzzles that each clue represents only increase my frustration and irritation, prompting me to find excuses to escape. I would rather engage in a psychological thriller when it comes to mystery-solving. The mysteries of the everyday challenge our brains, leading some of us to feel stressed while others find joy in the challenge of solving them.

Mystery is part of the fabric of life, presenting puzzles to a child, algebra challenges to a boy, new parents with dilemmas about their baby and the elderly with questions about their fading existence. Some mysteries are fun, others bearable, whilst yet other mysteries can be excruciatingly painful such as rejection or betrayal, leaving people feeling shattered and desperate. To navigate this world filled with stress, brokenness and pain means to embrace mystery as part of our daily lives.

I resonate with Aart van der Leeuw, the Dutch poet-philosopher, who states, "The mystery of life is not a problem to be solved, but a reality to be experienced." Embracing this profound perspective often leads to rich revelations from the mysteries woven into our lives. Mystery suggests that life is open-ended instead of completed, encouraging exploration of new thinking patterns, deeper experiences, spiritual moments, unexpected relationships and fresh insights. The specific mystery surrounding my husband's brain tumour has unfolded many new avenues for me. It has fostered a greater sense of patience in my naturally hurried self, transformed our social life from a limited circle of similar individuals to meeting all kinds of fascinating and diverse personalities and has brought novel and engaging work opportunities for us both. Furthermore, it has heightened my awareness of how nurturing a vital relationship with my body can cultivate peace and joy and undeniably, it has deepened my spiritual connection with God and the hopeful promise of eternity.

Therapists frequently encourage the attitude of curiosity for good reason, and I, too, urge readers to embrace this essential perspective. It empowers us in the presence of mystery and suffering instead of feeling entirely overwhelmed by it. Cultivating curiosity about challenges and mysteries can lead to insights and support. I worked with a client, Sarah, who felt completely detached from her life, perceiving it as if it were in black and white rather than the vibrant colours she once remembered. Her dissociation left both Sarah and I puzzled. However, as we approached the significant obstacle in her life with curiosity, the murky waters began to clear, revealing some clarity about the painful facts of her childhood. This understanding did not yield a straightforward solution but instead helped her confront and acknowledge the realities of her past. Over time, her dissociation faded, enabling her to reconnect with herself and fully experience both her past pain and her longing for a richer life. It was curiosity that served as the key to exploring the mystery and finding healing.

Mysteries can be emotional enigmas or spiritual struggles. My friend Tamsin grapples with the mysteries of faith, wondering when and how to interpret the Bible as literal, metaphorical, or mythical and how it is possible for God to be gendered. She questions how we can discern the Divine voice as distinctly different from our own. As we navigate these mysteries, she feels tempted to give up on God. However, as I reflect on my own faith experience, I realise that often, God has been enshrouded in mystery, but embracing this and fostering curiosity has led me to discover the Presence of God within the mystery; He reveals Himself in confusing and challenging situations simply as Presence, and not always with answers.

So much peace can be found by simply accepting that life has mysteries. I suggest there is goodness and gold hidden within all mysteries, from crosswords to relational challenges and even in deeper suffering. Initially, we must accept the mystery is real and present and then adopt curiosity. We cannot predict the discovery, but as we gently explore it, there will be a hidden treasure waiting to be mined, including Divine Presence. Exploring life's difficult mysteries means that we are fully real, present and alive within our own lives, and we can often find new answers and experiences leading to greater fulfilment.

———— ∞ ————
Practice

Take some breaths to settle.

Then, bring your awareness to your thoughts.

Do not analyse or judge them; just accept what you observe.

Then, bring your awareness to the specific emotions or general feelings that are present in you. Again, without analysing or judging, just stepping back to observe them.

Can you bring your awareness to the somatic feelings you have in your body?

Be curious about what is there, acknowledging and experiencing all things without judgement.

Stress

Two years after welcoming my much-wanted fourth child, I felt both fatigued and stressed. As I looked ahead to September, when she would begin part-time nursery, I anticipated a much-needed break. I envisioned doing all sorts of things for myself to help me restore and revitalise without the happy chaos of toddlers at my feet. However, this was the moment that James was unexpectedly diagnosed with a brain tumour, shattering any hope of rest. I thought I was already exhausted from caring much of the time single-handedly for four young kids, and had no idea a whole new level of demands and exhaustion was coming my way. Had I known the challenges ahead, I would have exclaimed, "There's no way I can handle this," like my instinctive reaction to running a marathon. Instead, I discovered ways to manage the exhaustion and stress.

I faced the ongoing challenges of motherhood and found strategies to manage my stress. I increased my running, partly to physically release the pent-up emotions. Additionally, I became more introspective, cherishing moments alone, often outdoors, allowing myself to simply be. This contemplative practice sparked a deeper interest in mindful movement, enriching my own traditional understanding of God in new and beautiful ways. By grounding myself in both the physical and spiritual realms, I expanded my capacity to handle stress, often feeling that I managed well, if not flawlessly.

We need to find ways to cope with stress and maintain our window of tolerance, as psychiatrist and neuroscientist Dan Siegel explains. The window of tolerance refers to the healthy zone where we can respond to stress without tipping into overwhelm (hyperarousal) or completely shutting down (hypoarousal). During challenging times, our window of tolerance is something we must protect and sustain to survive. Developing somatic and spiritual awareness significantly enhances our tolerance for stress and suffering, a fact supported by scientific research and reflected in my own experience.

Leaning into somatic and spiritual awareness significantly helps us manage stress.

Firstly, when we pay attention to our bodies, we are helpfully pulled out of our anxious minds that spiral out of control and into something real and present. This allows us to feel grounded and calmer as we live in the moment. If we tend to shut down in stress, feeling detached or even dissociated from ourselves, then awareness of our bodies is a means of reconnecting with the life that our beating hearts and breathing lungs constantly remind us of. Thus, awareness of our body brings us into the present moment, the here and now and the current of vitality and peace that flows in and through each of us.

Secondly, we can give attention to the spiritual dimension of life. Becoming aware of the existential reasons you have for living: your family, a purpose in life and the Divine plan are ways of consciously expanding your awareness beyond the immediate challenge that is dysregulating you and causing stress. Spiritual awareness helps us remember that there is more to life than our current struggles and there is more to life than just me—there is a wider, deeper, vaster experience of life beyond ourselves and this includes the Presence of the Divine and a whole and holy purpose and plan. This existential or transcendent awareness, as Frankl insists, can ground us in something far bigger than our own experience, as stressful and difficult as it might be.

To become whole, spiritual and somatic awareness can support us when we navigate the tumultuous waters of stress and uncertainty. These two dimensions bring stability and peace and can enable us to be resilient in challenges.

———— ✿ ————

Practice

Bring your awareness to your breath, noticing its rhythm and depth. Maybe listen to the sound of your breath or inaudibly say in and out or even count the breath to help you focus. This may help your body relax.

As you breathe in, invite the Divine Presence to come and be with you and in your life.

As you breathe out, release difficult emotions and tensions to the Divine.

Continue with this intentional breath prayer for as long as you wish.

Lost

Sometimes, mystery and stress can overwhelm us to the point where we can't make sense of anything and feel somewhat lost. The pathway to wholeness is not a linear journey from A to B; rather, it weaves through life's complexities, enabling us to grow from the inside out.

I remember James and I attending marriage counselling sessions with a lovely couple, Guy and Tania, to make sense of the mystery of our new normal several years ago. As I explained the complexities of James's health and its effects, we all agreed that there wasn't yet a map for a situation like ours. I certainly felt lost and wondered what I could expect from our marriage, which had been profoundly affected by physical, cognitive and emotional changes. What could we expect from our marriage? What could I expect from James? How could James still seem to expect our marriage to remain the same when, for me, it simply wasn't? There was a lot of confusion as I questioned how I could admit to struggling when I had my health and four wonderful children and besides, my husband had survived and wasn't that amazing, as everyone told me. His incredible resilience and positivity which was rightly recognised, made it feel wrong for me to acknowledge my own struggles. The silence of many people regarding my experience was most likely intended to honour my husband's efforts but left me perplexed and upset as I questioned my own identity and experience which had been dramatically affected. After James's first surgery, I felt as though I had a husband back who had been in a severe accident, someone who never fully recovered. Feeling gratitude and positivity weren't natural responses to a devastating reality.

One day I painted how I felt to try and make sense of everything I've just described. The result was a small smudge of a silhouetted figure floating in the middle of a cave-like space surrounded by broad, haphazard brushstrokes in every direction. I can still sense how I felt at that time as I visualise the painting: uncertain, lost and lonely.

None of us likes to be lost, as feelings of loneliness and powerlessness can emerge. You may recall a specific memory of being lost as a child or an adult, or perhaps you have a generalised awareness of a time when you felt lost. Lostness occurs when predictable pathways disappear, forcing us to work hard to make sense of new and unfamiliar territory. As I write, it is the beginning of Lent, which marks forty days of lostness for the devotee, during which we choose to relinquish our automatic ways of living and set aside our everyday crutches to open ourselves to the transcendent truths of the spiritual realm. Many biblical stories recount people wandering in the wilderness, where they felt lost. This includes Jesus, who allowed himself to be led into the desert, severing all connections with the familiar. This is what getting lost entails: disconnection from the familiar.

Experiencing life without a map in unfamiliar terrain and without knowing where you are meant to be going is challenging. But it invites a new awareness. Sometimes, it is not about rushing out of the discomfort of uncertainty and the vulnerability that comes with being lost, but rather about embracing this state of lostness. Much like Jesus, we may find ourselves becoming more resilient through our time in the desert, drawing strength from spiritual nourishment. A new perspective might begin to emerge, revealing a sense of Divine Presence accompanying us in the wilderness and perhaps we will experience being found by the Divine rather than having to find our own way in our isolation.

The pathway to wholeness encourages us to acknowledge our lostness while offering a way through the mystery and suffering to a greater sense of wholeness.

Practice

Settle yourself by bringing your awareness to your breath.

Imagine, using any of your physical senses, that you are in a desert.

What do you see and hear? What do you smell? How do you sense the heat and cold of the desert around you?

As you are there, you see a figure walking towards you. As he comes close you see it is the person of Jesus.

What does he look like? How do you feel?

Does he say anything to you or convey anything to you about your experience in the desert?

Be with the silence, or the conversation sensing what comes to you in this situation.

Loss

"To live is to be willing to die over and over again," says Buddhist teacher Pema Chodron, and how true this is. Loss, which signifies the end of things, is a part of everyday life. It occurs in small ways, such as when we misplace our keys or when a friendship begins to fade. Loss happens when we leave the comfort of home, when our children move on, or when the slow stealth of ageing takes away our youth. We may also recognise loss in significant events, like when we lose a job, our health, or someone we loved deeply. Loss is a harsh reality of life, one we are often ill-equipped to handle.

The corresponding emotion to loss is grief, although many people find grief a difficult emotion.

There are various responses to loss. Some individuals adopt an unsustainable positivity, seeking only the silver linings to avoid the reality of loss and the pain it brings. Over the past thirteen years, many well-meaning people have happily glossed over the realities of James's and my loss, expressing emphatic gratitude that the tumour was found, that it was operable, that he didn't lose his sight entirely, or that he managed to work, skimming over the enormous losses endured and still being faced. Positivity is helpful but not when it denies reality. If we can't live in reality, then our experience of life isn't real. Another response is to focus solely on our grief to the extent of becoming depressed and it is not easy. We need to find a way of dealing with loss that is wise and that enables wholeness to emerge.

"Grieve and move on", this wonderful refrain was repeated by a teacher, Ray Mayhew, who battled chronic illness himself. I heard it several years after

James had transitioned to his new normal following surgery and radiotherapy. While many people tried to exude positivity and hope, I often felt isolated in my grief over the losses we faced. Being encouraged to grieve felt like much-needed permission and I began to accept that I could grieve and that I didn't need to stay in this forever. As a therapist now, I understand that if we fail to process our emotions, they can become trapped within us, leading to bitterness and can negatively affect our wellbeing.

"If we don't transform our pain, we will most assuredly transmit it," says Franciscan writer Richard Rohr, offering us a slightly more sophisticated version of the aphorism, "Hurt people, hurt people." When we don't process our pain, our hurts and our grief, then the brokenness we have experienced will remain part of us so that we become broken, too. Sue was in a partnership with Steve for over twenty years, but she came for counselling as the relationship had broken down and Steve had had enough of her. Sue described the relationship and her life patterns that emerged from a traumatic childhood with a mother who had Paranoid Personality Disorder, which she had never processed. We realised that she was sometimes acting towards Steve in a way her mother had treated her, with harsh words, screaming and anxiety that was out of control in their relationship. It took two years to transform her pain and end her transmitting it into her marriage. Losses of any kind need to be acknowledged, accepted as such and responded to with the emotion of grief. And then we can move on.

I've noticed how my children growing up and needing me less is a true loss for me. Motherhood has been a significant yet unexpected blessing in my life, bringing me much joy and fun with my kids alongside the hard work it has also created. But my purpose and identity have become intertwined with this role. I realise that their presence and needs have offered me anchors on multiple levels as I've had to, and also wanted to, find energy and meaning in being a mother and very often father to them too. As they fly the nest, I am tempted to live in denial and to fill the void with constant activity. As the kids come and go from home, my heart yo-yos between excitement and sadness. However, I am learning to grieve the losses and to embrace the mystery of the next phase of life, which holds new blessings.

Denial and depression are unhelpful and so is transmitting our pain to others. But as we accept our losses and grieve them, we can move on, finding peace and wholeness.

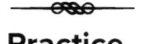

Practice

Settle yourself

Is there a loss that comes to mind now?

As you hold it in your awareness, can you feel a corresponding somatic response (maybe you have sensations in your heart or stomach)?

Wherever you feel the grief of loss, take a moment to acknowledge it, to hold it.

Then take your breath to that place in your body and surround the felt sense with your breath. You could even take a hand to this part of your body or hug yourself to bring comfort to the pain or sadness.

Use the exhale to let go of some of the grief.

Use the exhale to release your grief to the Divine Presence that is always and already with you and around you.

Suffering

There are mysteries and losses that are unbearable and not easily alleviated. While I have known some degree of stress, struggle and suffering, it doesn't compare to close friends who have lost three out of five children. They lost each of these precious children two years apart between 2001 and 2005 to three separate illnesses that struck suddenly. There was very little, if any, warning of the impending loss of each child, and each time, it was a devastating blow that left the parents and the communities around them reeling. They say time is a healer, but this level of loss and grief will remain with them throughout their lives.

When words fail to comfort us in the face of devastating loss, what can we do? Is there a chance for hope once more? Can we ever feel whole again? Although the hurt and vivid memories may linger, a path toward wholeness exists. It doesn't solely involve fixing ourselves; rather, it's about allowing our broken selves to be embraced by others frequently. "A burden shared is a burden halved", the saying goes. The internal disconnection brought about by suffering disrupts our sense of stability, yet we can find solace when others come together to share that pain. The African concept of "*Ubuntu*" translates to "I am because we are," encapsulating the essence of belonging and support through relationships with others. "What makes something better is connection," agrees Brené Brown. Connection with others to alleviate grief is commonly said to help the grieving.

Many religions provide a ready-made community of support for people experiencing suffering. However, Christianity has at its heart a God who suffers with us, offering compassionate understanding and connection during our struggles.

Jürgen Moltmann, who recently passed away, was a notable German theologian known for his work on 'The Crucified God.' He shifted centuries of doctrinal emphasis from viewing the cross as a mere mechanical operation for salvation to understanding that God is a being who suffers alongside us. Writing partly in response to the atrocities of the Holocaust, he articulated how God is forever intertwined with the full human experience, including suffering. I can't express how the suffering of Jesus—his misunderstanding, betrayal, torture and death—has impacted me during my moments of grief. While I do not wish to compare my experience to the pain of grieving parents or Holocaust survivors, it has nonetheless been a grief that I have known and had to confront. When I have faced walls of uncertainty and sadness, not only regarding my situation but also concerning the suffering of others, I find comfort and peace in knowing that God also suffered. If God could allow Himself to endure spiritual, emotional and physical suffering on the cross, then I can trust that my personal sufferings will also hold meaning. I can also anticipate resurrection and resolution one day.

So often silent presence is the best way to console someone who is really suffering. As people hold our hands and cry with us, this bodily human presence consoles the grieving in times of unavoidable suffering. The spirituality of suffering is that we might become more connected; connected to a wider body of people and connected to a suffering God who suffers with us.

The pathway of wholeness is a sacred and healing journey for those who suffer. It invites communal sharing and fosters awareness of the broader, deeper and more profound love of the Divine, who experienced human suffering for all people and throughout all time.

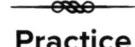

Practice

Sit back on a sofa or even lie on a comfy bed.

Allow the physical experience of being surrounded and held to speak to your whole being about feeling supported and held.

Bring to mind those people who have offered you support in times of trouble.

You can extend this somatic awareness and your mental memories of being supported and held to an awareness to the One who holds you in his hands, suffering with you and holding you with love and hope.

Chapter 8

Beautiful Romance

Beauty has an intriguing connection to suffering, and many people, myself included, have found that experiencing suffering somehow enhances our capacity to perceive beauty. Beauty softens the blows of the harsh world we inhabit and alleviates the weight of sadness in our souls. However, beauty is not superfluous, like an unnecessary luxury, nor is it merely a crutch to lean on in times of trouble; rather, beauty is essential to our wellbeing and wholeness. The desire for beauty reflects a longing for goodness and truth in life. Ancient, medieval and modern philosophers have all recognised the significance of beauty in infusing human existence with meaning and that it is deeply connected to goodness and truth.

We find longing and desire everywhere in our culture for beautiful things, whether they be the shiny new car, the lithe and lovely featured woman or the dreamy home. Romance may seem an odd term to use, but beauty allures us and we can fall in love with her when we encounter her. Our love for beauty can, of course, transform into lust, which is a corruption of longing and love; yet, there is nonetheless a desire to experience beauty, to behold her and to know her intimately.

All of us constantly long for beauty, whether we seek it in things or in others. We also want to exhibit our own beauty so that others will admire, affirm and be attracted to us. Medieval philosopher Thomas Aquinas explains that "Beauty is that which pleases upon being seen." Beauty is something perceived with the senses and felt in the soul, drawing us toward it. The pursuit of beauty is an everyday part of life, a mysterious one perhaps, but its presence is something that vivifies our lives and souls.

Can you think of something beautiful—a person, a place, or an object—that you would call beautiful? Are you aware of how you have desired to behold this beauty, to be captivated by it and drawn into an experience of it so that it touches you at a deeper level of your being? Beauty is attractive, which may seem obvious, but it does pull us toward it, creating a relational and romantic element where we want to approach it and connect with it more profoundly, more intimately. In this way, beauty romances us and draws us into union.

Women have extensive knowledge about beauty, often regarded as the more beautiful sex. This generalisation has its roots in the way beautiful and woman are frequently paired, leading to a long-standing recognition of women's beauty. Regardless of the reasons, women often aspire to enhance their appeal. For centuries, the age-old cosmetic industry has catered predominantly to women's aesthetics. Women have adorned themselves in elegant and stylish clothing, incorporating various makeup styles, driven either by innate desires or the pursuit of attracting men. While this pursuit can sometimes border on excess, women maintain a complex and somewhat ambivalent relationship with beauty. Women have also tended to be characterised as more romantic than men. Whether it's a desire to be swept off their feet by the archetypal knight in shining armour or weeping over romance novels, women are often considered more romantic than men. However, beauty and being romanced by beauty are not superficial or sentimental, they are vital aspects of all human existence.

Dante expresses in The Divine Comedy, "The beauty I witnessed surpasses all human thought, beyond our mortal limitations—and I am completely engulfed in it," highlighting a vision of Divine beauty in Paradiso. Our attraction to beauty elevates us beyond our individual selves, fostering a spiritual connection with something greater. Beauty, in its various manifestations, inspires a deep longing to experience it, to connect with it and even be overawed and in union with it, allowing us to absorb this beauty and become beautiful ourselves.

One scripture that I have cherished teaches, "By beholding God's glory [His overwhelming beauty, truth and goodness], we are transformed into that same glory." Beauty captivates us, drawing us toward itself and instilling a desire to unite with it and become one with it. Medieval theologians emphasised a threefold mystical path to the Divine: first, spiritual cleansing, followed by spiritual illumination, and culminating in union with God. This connection is experienced by Christians worldwide, albeit in less technical language than in Medieval times. Allowing ourselves to be captivated by beauty, to behold it and merge with it, is a profound spiritual encounter with the Divine. Thus, a romance with Divine Beauty is part of our journey towards wholeness.

Beauty from Ashes

Our experience of beauty can deepen as a result of suffering.

"There is a crack in everything, that's how the light gets in." I didn't come across these words in Leonard Cohen's song until recently, but they beautifully describe my own experience after James lost his sight and health. I felt the pain of loss and confusion at the new normal, and my former way of understanding the world seemed somewhat fragmented. It was as though a large fissure had opened up in the ground of my soul.

However, when I felt the most vulnerable to pain, I also felt the most open to beauty; there was now a broader access point for beauty to be perceived within me. I would stop and gaze at a tree in blossom or hear classical music playing and be moved to tears. It was as though the pain I experienced had also opened me up to moments of beauty. The cracks enable the light to penetrate our fractured souls. Don Saliers, a liturgical scholar explains how there is an integral link between grace and suffering and how true beauty often emerges in the tension between these forces.

"...beauty instead of ashes..." This little line comes from the Bible and speaks of how beauty is offered in exchange for the ashes of mourning, loss and destruction experienced by the Hebrews. Or we might talk about the phoenix rising from the ashes, to describe the possibility for beauty in the times of the darkest despair. Simone Weil, the twentieth-century mystic, writes in her book 'Gravity and Grace', how extreme affliction, including physical pain, distress of soul and social degradation, creates a state which is the equivalent of death. She continues that those who can withstand it, can return from it and indeed rise from the dead. This is an experience of the triumph of beauty over suffering.

The metaphysical dimension of beauty emerges from the idea of rising from the dead, where life surpasses death and beauty overcomes destruction. This core message is clearly reflected in Jesus' life. The cross, being the most depicted symbol throughout history, can become so familiar that its profound significance —beauty overcoming destruction—can fade from our perception. Through the suffering of God, vividly portrayed on the cross, we witness the beauty of the Divine nature: the gentleness towards creation, the mercy for human faults, the compassion for our brokenness and the loving embrace that invites healing. Hans Urs von Balthasar encapsulates the paradox of beauty unveiled in the suffering of the cross, stating that the Crucified [radiates] the splendour of the Divine beauty—a beauty that is rooted in love to the point of self-emptying.

A thirsty and dying man hanging on a wooden structure 2000 years ago might not be the image we immediately associate with beauty. However, if we seek a pathway that guides us through the entirety of life, where some endure insufferable pain and we hope to find meaning in our existence, I suggest this image serves as a powerful means to connect suffering with beauty, where beauty triumphs.

Beauty captivates us in a way that hard factual truth cannot. It draws us into union with the Divine, whilst also revealing truth. In the last two lines of 'Ode on a Grecian Urn', the poet John Keats presents the well-known words,

"Beauty is truth, truth beauty—that is all.

Ye know on earth and all ye need to know."

In other words, beauty is all we need to uncover truth, and truth is inherently beautiful. Beauty and truth support us in times of difficulty. The truth of beauty may be recognised as the Divine image within a person, the sublime sweetness of a violin solo or God's sacrificial love on a wooden cross.

Experiencing beauty is vital for human flourishing, it reminds us of who we are and who the Divine Creator is and in this experiential knowledge, we become more whole.

———⊶⊶———
Practice

Do one or all of the following:

Listen to something beautiful and gentle, maybe a classical piece. Sense into how beauty makes you feel as it is conveyed through sound.

View a beautiful work of art to sense beauty through sight. Smell a beautiful aroma, to experience beauty in an olfactory way.

Contemplate that these somatic experiences of beauty might open up a way of knowing the Divine as ultimately beautiful.

Gentle Wonder

Beauty invites an emotional response on our part, it can inspire awe and evoke wonder.

There's a short little book, 'Gift from the Sea', written by Anne Morrow Lindbergh, a mother of six, reflecting on a brief vacation at the seashore. She wonders how the gentleness of the sea, the beauty of the sand and seashells and the presence of the warm sun speak to and replenish her. When I read this over 10 years ago, it resonated deeply with me as I, too, was fatigued and fragmented under the responsibility of all I had to do, and her writing invited me into the same contemplation of how certain aspects of nature offered a gentle and restorative beauty. It further awakened my mystical leanings, where I had already found resources and the

Divine presence in everyday things from running bath water to torrential stormy rain.

Beauty surrounds us, some of it sings brightly and boldly through sunflowers, while other forms are more subtle, evoking gentle wonder. Some beauty is hidden or fleeting, and unless we slow down, we will miss it, like the delicate structure of a snowflake or brief rays of light through cloudy skies. Awareness of these gentler forms of beauty in people, places and nature enriches our lives, bringing comfort and peace.

My neighbour Stephen recently passed away from cancer at the age of 76. He was a beautiful man with a gentle soul. He spent part of his life as the head rose gardener in Regent's Park and was a very knowledgeable horticulturist. His garden was a narrow strip of land, yet he planted over two hundred different species, with a few meandering gravel pathways that allowed visitors like me to browse and admire. We would visit each other, alternating venues between his beautiful, flourishing garden and my rather barren garden, which had only hedges at the border. He began to teach me his craft and helped me plant three flowerbeds in my garden. Every encounter with him outdoors was an experience of gentleness and beauty, and I found myself calmer and enriched after our time together.

People hold beauty in their character, and perhaps there is someone who has impacted you with their gentleness and kind affection. Maybe an aunt, grandparent or teacher who demonstrated a quiet beauty. Or can you think of moments where you've been calmed and comforted perhaps by the quiet beauty of a summer's evening or listening to a bird sing? These experiences cause us to behold everyday beauty that can be an experience of 'everyday mysticism.' Or as Simone Weil puts it, "The beauty of the world is Christ's tender smile for us, coming through matter."

I have learnt to slow down and appreciate the quieter moments of beauty and wonder as otherwise we don't recognise them when they are right with us. We can take everyday experiences and adopt a sensory, mindful approach to experience ordinary beauty in more extraordinary ways. By cultivating a mindful awareness of beauty in everyday life, we ground our bodies and souls and we can also enhance our spiritual awareness of how Divine Beauty manifests through matter to inspire and love us.

Practice

The Examen was devised by Ignatius of Loyola in the sixteenth century to help followers recognise moments of beauty and blessing in the everyday:

Reflect on your past 24 hours.

Where did you sense the consolations incidents that moved you towards Divine goodness, beauty and truth?

Where did you sense the desolations moments that took you away from Divine goodness, beauty and truth?

Linger over the consolations aware of the comfort they bring to you now giving thanks for them.

Majestic Awe

Beauty can be so awe-inspiring and powerful that it sometimes cannot be described by words or can cause us to even weep. Wide savanna landscapes extending to the horizon, majestic mountain ranges and vast starry skies exemplify this kind of striking beauty. To the embarrassment of my children, I sometimes cry when planes take off! This incredible demonstration of human engineering, combined with the powerful sensory experience of energy, can evoke an overwhelming sense of beauty and power.

As we moved into our new home after the year of trials, we had a wonderful view out through the bottom left corner of our garden. There was a fence marking off the house just below us, which obscured over half of the view, but nonetheless, there was a sizeable window upstairs with a view of undulating hills. It was awe-inspiring and our bedroom led to a small decked area which became a favourite spot to sit and drink tea or meditate. But alas, our neighbour Carly, despite her welcome, had planning permission for an extension that our solicitor had missed. After one year, up went her annexe, brick by brick, until a raft of parallel gables finally obscured my precious view. I felt utterly bereft of my daily fix of beauty and had to find it on dogwalks instead.

Another cherished view I have enjoyed is by the sea. To escape the stress of sunburn, sandy bottoms and sandwich-making, on English seaside holidays when the children were young, I would take myself daily to a nearby headland by foot or car. Here I could gaze out beyond the lovely white lighthouse to the expansive ocean. The light and water were different each time: sometimes rough with murmuring currents, sometimes sparkling on a gentle sea and sometimes flat with soft sunsets. Yet, every purposeful visit provided me with an experience of awe and beauty. The stunning scene before me lifted me away from my minor concerns, allowing me to appreciate something compelling and captivating beyond my own concerns.

As we encounter the beautiful, the majestic and the powerful in ways that are not destructive, we realise that there is something bigger than us in this world. Something more powerful, more majestic and more beautiful. I suggest the appropriate response is an awe and wonder that reminds us of a bigger reality. To encounter beauty is to be pulled towards the object of beauty which then pulls us beyond ourselves to an experience of transcendence.

Experiencing beauty can be profoundly spiritual, lifting us beyond our limitations and pain. Our awareness broadens, enabling us to become more than we are now. We find awe and wonder in both the subtle, concealed beauty of the world and its grand, powerful manifestations. By appreciating beauty, our lives broaden, making us more beautiful and more whole.

Practice

Practice awe this week:

Take yourself somewhere where you can see or experience something of power and majesty. Find a fast-flowing river, an expansive view or listen to a dramatic piece of music that stirs the emotions. If this is not possible, close your eyes and use your imagination.

As you engage with it, sense the beauty and majesty of the experience. How do you feel it in your body? Be aware of your somatic response with particular sensations or a general feeling.

Widen your awareness of how this experience might be speaking to you of the Divine Nature.

Desire

What is your response to the word desire? Beauty and romance touch upon the realm of desire, which can arouse different responses. In modern culture, desire is closely associated with sex and consumerism. We need only to view the TV series 'Love Island' to witness the incitement of desire that leads to casual sex, or 'The Traitors', where contestants are stirred with the desire to win status and prize money at any cost.

St Augustine, a notable Church Father, distinguished between disordered desire (lust) and ordered desire (love). I suggest our culture has become increasingly disordered, promoting self-centred pleasure, power and material acquisition that can leave us feeling used, unfulfilled and empty, rather than fostering the desires that enable our growth and well-being. We are all susceptible to corrupted desires that leave us wanting. Have you experienced the desire for new clothes or material things, which, once acquired, turned out to be unremarkable? Or the desire for a sexual high through physical encounters or pornography, which might afterwards lead to a profound sense of emptiness? Or the desire to get one up on someone who has offended, only to discover it is an endless ladder of brokenness that leads nowhere? The wrong kind of desire can land us in a desolate no man's land at best and surrounded by destruction at worst.

"Desire is not in itself wrong, but it must be rightly ordered." The orderly desire that Augustine speaks of is directed towards goodness and the source of beauty, goodness and truth. Whilst I've fallen in love humanely speaking and had access to material possessions, the earthly experiences of desire towards temporal things and even people don't really satisfy in the same way that I have experienced desire in an ordered or spiritual way.

I developed a meditation app in 2015, dedicating over a year to writing and recording its content. I felt immense pride in what I had created, especially with the insights that informed the meditations. My central idea was that, through self-discovery, we are constantly seeking meaning. The craftsman wants to create or repair, the drunkard seeks humour and escape, the scholar craves understanding and the model desires to be beautiful. We are all, through ordered or disordered means, desiring something currently out of our grasp. To have desire is part of being human. However, we can choose to what end our desire leads us.

I suggest we direct them toward that which holds ultimate value, the Ultimate Transcendent One. We often separate the spiritual from our everyday experiences of longing and desire, believing that ethical behaviour and the right attitude are more important. What I find intriguing about spiritual desire is that while it leads us toward the Divine, the desire itself is a means of experiential knowing. As we cultivate a desire for the Divine, the very experience of that desire brings the Divine Presence to us. As Rowan Williams, the former Archbishop of Canterbury, explains, "Desire is not a gap which God has yet to fill; it is itself the presence of God at work in us."

We can channel our desires towards the appropriate objects: shifting focus from ourselves, our status, clothes and possessions and transcending the desire for earthly matters, even people, towards the Divine. Regardless of our form of agnosticism or faith, we can steer our desire toward Divine Beauty to enhance our spirituality and become more holy and whole.

Practice

Awareness of Desire:

Are you able to bring to mind something that captivates your attention, or can you bring up the feeling of desire? You are welcome to bring to mind anything that connects you with the feeling of desire, (even sexual desire). Feel into the presence of desire and how you experience it in your heart, mind, soul and also your body.

Allow this felt sense of desire to detach from the everyday object, person, project or thing and contemplate how this desire might be rightly directed towards the Divine. You may stop here with a simple cognitive awareness.

Or maybe you are comfortable taking it a stage further and actually directing this desire towards the Divine. However, you understand Him.

As you direct your desire towards God, perhaps you are gently aware of the presence of God within your desire, as Rowan Williams suggests.

Union

I've been intrigued by sex for many years! It was another embarrassment for my kids when I recently declared that we are all sexual beings as they grimaced at the idea older people might actually still engage in sexual activity! Sex and sexuality are fascinating subjects and people are obsessed with them for a reason and I've wanted to understand why. That is one reason I took a module in my

Master's program entitled 'Sexuality and Spirituality'. At last, I thought, someone is going to tell me why God created sex and what it really means. However, I must admit, the module felt like an anticlimax, as it preferred to explore the gender and sex debate more than discuss the meaning of human sexual drives. I am still amazed at how little spiritual literature exists within the Christian field on this universally captivating topic.

However, the Bible does address desire, romance and sexuality in the 'Song of Songs'. This small book, located at the centre of the Bible, is often easy to overlook. In Orthodox Jewish communities, young boys were generally advised against reading it due to its sensual imagery. While it may seem mild compared to the sexual themes found in modern literature, it certainly captures a subtle yet genuine eroticism in the interactions between the lover and the beloved. This lengthy poem portrays the romantic yearnings of a couple, characterised by both emotional and physical attraction and strongly suggests sexual engagement with each other. Most interpretations will say it is an allegory for God's love for humanity in a particular or generalised way. My experience of reading this book instilled in me a desire for a rightly-ordered longing toward God, leading me to believe that spiritual desire could supplant earthly romance and for a few years, I even aspired to remain single because of this.

Just as human connection finds something ultimate in sexual union, I suggest that union is also the goal of the spiritual life. The mystic writers grasped this clearly and the Medieval Threefold Path taught a progressive pathway from purification, to enlightenment, to union with God. Julian of Norwich has written one of the most profound mystical texts in history and coined the term oneing to describe this union, or one-ness where the soul is united with God. She writes, "The soul is preciously knit to Him...in its endless joying in Him." The spiritual experience of union or oneing is also traced in the later writings of another mystic woman, Teresa of Avila, in the sixteenth century, who talks about this union bringing about a state of spiritual ecstasy when she is consumed by the great love of God. Some of her descriptions suggest her experience of Divine intimacy was intense in the same way sexual union can be.

Using the words God, desire, union and ecstasy in the same sentence could unsettle the reader and yet sex and spirituality are a vital part of the human experience. Our everyday experiences are full of Divine grace and our bodies are sacred, and desire can be rightly ordered. Jesus speaks about there being a wedding and a marriage feast at the end of earthly time where Christ will be united with the bride. This union is far from the hellish orgy-type scene painted by Hieronymous Bosch, centuries ago. There will be something beautiful, redeemed, whole and holy about this union with the Divine in eternity, but I suggest we might have pointers towards this holistic union right now in the everyday existence of sex. If we can rightly order our longing and desire towards the Divine we are somewhere on the way to becoming more whole.

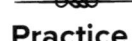

Practice

You might want to explore the meaning in these words from the Song of Songs and then meditate on them:

Read "Let him kiss me with the kisses of his mouth—for your love is more delightful than wine."

Reflect "Let him kiss me with the kisses of his mouth—for your love is more delightful than wine."

Respond "Let him kiss me with the kisses of his mouth—for your love is more delightful than wine."

Receive "Let him kiss me with the kisses of his mouth—for your love is more delightful than wine."

Chapter 9

Vulnerable Surrender

Paradox is often present when we explore spirituality, where beauty is found through suffering, treasure is hidden and physical bodies hold the key to spiritual truths. So often, we seek something better beyond ourselves and overlook the treasures that may be hidden within our very lives, buried in our suffering, in the earth, or within our bodies. Instead of emphasising intellectual knowledge and actions aimed at achieving external goals, we must turn this paradigm upside down to become more whole. If the life we long for resides in the life we are already living, then there is another paradox we need to embrace: that of vulnerability and surrender. Embracing vulnerability and surrendering to our lives can lead to peace and fulfilment.

Vulnerability is likely more in vogue these days than surrender, which still carries a certain hangover in this season of women's liberation. I've brought up the word surrender in discussions, and I often notice a slight recoil, particularly from women. I understand this, as the word can easily trigger personal or generational memories of the imposed submission that has long been placed on women. Thomas Laquer, in 'Making Sex: Body and Gender from the Greeks to Freud', explains the Ancient Greek one-sex model, where the male is the standard and the female is seen as derivative, passive and receptive. This perspective has subtly extended through centuries of patriarchal culture. In many eras and locations, women have not chosen their destiny; rather, they have been directed by and are dependent on their fathers, husbands or the patriarchal structures in place having to submit to them. Within this paradigm, women have held an intrinsic understanding that they are not the providers but are instead recipients of male provision, whether it be money, housing, social standing or sperm. Women's identity and survival have depended on male provision, making them vulnerable to exploitation or denial. While receiving provision from others can be a blessing, it can also be frustrating for women to have to surrender to male dominance and painful to feel vulnerable to the preferences of those who control their lives.

Whilst times have changed, I knew something of the silent surrender to the preferences of others. My husband and I both came from more traditional families providing a model of female domesticity and male provision. My husband expected his life plan, his job and his preferences to prevail. Marrying young at just 23 I was hopeful and somewhat naive, and I wanted to do exciting things with my degree and with my life. However, the traditional paradigm was affirmed by the vicar who married us suggesting that I did not work in the first year of our marriage so I could be around for James in his teacher's holidays! I submitted to this without challenging it, but I became disillusioned and discontent.

There was a quiet dismissal of my potential to possess a purpose beyond being a wife and mother that could in any way compromise my husband's vocation. It was deeply painful and at odds with my expectations as I stood at the threshold of feminist hope, yet I was held back by my own submission to a patriarchal paradigm that didn't encourage women's talents and aspirations. A combination of culture and my agreement with this model kept me in silent submission. However, while this has very much changed, I have also learnt something valuable about surrender. I realise I have a choice and that I can either choose change or to accept circumstances as some things cannot be avoided; this acceptance and surrender can release me from resentment and needless frustration.

There is something to be mined from women's familiar struggle with vulnerability, receptivity and surrender. Choosing surrender is not the same as imposed submission; rather surrender is the selective submission of self for a greater cause. We might do this when we submit to a new diet or exercise regime or when we defer present gratification by saving rather than spending our money. Being discerningly vulnerable we can find healing from our stress, struggles and sufferings. Intentional passivity and receptivity can open up a wider perspective and greater resourcing in our lives.

We can frame this another way by asking, what is the antidote for the stressful life and mental health issues of today? One response is to invite people to accept their own vulnerabilities so they may find healing, to surrender all the demands from without and within to find peace and to be receptive to everyday graces. Our patriarchal paradigms might have created some problems for women but there are answers hidden in the experience of women that can be redeemed and be resources for all of us.

Our society has adopted what I consider to be a distinctly masculine approach to problem-solving and success. The goal is often perceived as being out there on the horizon, requiring us to utilise our agency and intellect to find resolution. This approach needs to be balanced with a shifting perspective, where answers are hidden within this life, our bodies and our circumstances. Employing somatic and spiritual ways of knowing can allow us to be receptive to the hidden treasures in our daily lives. Instead of perpetually being active agents busying ourselves constantly, we can learn to embrace everyday life, to be vulnerable to our pain and need to surrender and release what isn't beneficial and receive the treasure that is already available to us.

I can struggle to apply this very wisdom. At times I prefer my efficiency and agency to vulnerable surrender and receptivity, racing around, trying to achieve everything myself and getting absolutely exhausted along the way. However, adopting a more receptive posture that allows for vulnerability and surrender can lead us to greater peace in life and enjoyment of it.

Vulnerable Humility

Vulnerability and humility can be beautiful to behold.

The 2017 version of Beauty and the Beast stars Emma Watson as the courageous Belle, who refuses to be bullied by the cold, arrogant and resentful Beast. Belle first arrives and is treated with rage and impatience as the Beast holds her prisoner in his castle. However, Belle stands her ground, surprising the Beast, who begins to drop his defences as they read and talk together, sharing their pain. As the Beast removes his mask of hostility, it is replaced by a softer, humbler self. In true Hollywood style, this iconic storyline concludes with the evil spell being broken and love blossoming between the Beast and Belle. This story of beauty emerging from the beastly is an archetypal narrative of love and beauty winning through. The key lies in the surrender of the Beast's prideful, angry exterior, where humility allows vulnerability to unfold, facilitating healing and transformation.

Our culture rarely promotes humility; consumerist systems encourage our boastful claims and prideful desires. Humility isn't shiny or Instagram-worthy. It may seem to denigrate the everyday as something dowdy, with self-effacing people leading drab lives. However, we all recognise the beauty of a truly humble person, as we have seen in figures like Gandhi or Mandela, or in the person of Jesus through the pages of the Bible. Humility is not the same as humiliation. Humiliation is inflicted upon a person to intimidate and shame them, while humility is a personal choice to remove the mask and embrace vulnerability, much like the Beast did.

Studying Theology as an undergraduate, I was often asked if my faith was rocked by the academic challenges. I remember one tutorial where it was just myself and the highly esteemed Professor of Buddhist Studies at that time. He was in his 60s and had decades of learning behind him, whereas I was 19 and unfamiliar with Buddhism. As he deconstructed my Christian worldview like a cat might play with a mouse just for the fun of it, I sat and squirmed. I couldn't wait to get out of the room. However, over time, I came to realise that the Divine is not apprehended through the intellect but rather is known experientially and through humility. Like many, I struggle with humility, but I have found it opens up new experiences of learning and healing.

The posture of humility is courageous. It strips us of our fragile securities and identities and opens us up to our vulnerabilities. Bréne Brown has been nicknamed the Godmother of vulnerability, and she says, "Vulnerability sounds like truth and feels like courage. Truth and courage aren't always comfortable, but they're never weakness." Admitting the truth and experiencing vulnerability is a brave thing, and it can mean that healing can begin.

A client, Susan, came to me because she was experiencing burnout. She was a social worker, well-respected for her 30-year career. She was really anxious as she shared her story and it became clear that a significant reason for her exhaustion was her struggle to acknowledge that she also had needs. We worked to dismantle the belief that she had to meet everyone else's needs to the point of exhaustion. Her identity as a carer at work and at home for her family allowed her to avoid confronting her own vulnerable feelings of unworthiness. It took time for her to recognise her humanity, accept that she had vulnerabilities and needs, and adopt a more reasonable view of herself, realising that she didn't need to martyr herself to feel good about herself.

Her story resonates with my own and with many women I encounter in therapy. Cultural paradigms push us all toward being the best we can be, but women, in particular, are burdened with caring for family, work colleagues, extended family, friends and the entire local community. Or so we convince ourselves. Acknowledging our own needs, brokenness, pain and limitations requires humility. However, a humble acceptance of our vulnerabilities allows us to receive help and restores wholeness in our lives.

Practice

Where are you feeling weak and vulnerable at the moment?

Bring your awareness to this. Maybe you can even notice it in your body?

Stay with this and bring some self-compassion to what you are feeling.

Breathe in the strength of the Divine Presence.

As you exhale out, receive this Strengthening Presence in your whole being.

Choiceful Surrender

My mother frequently tells me to let the river flow, possibly quoting Bob Dylan without realising it and she always adds, and don't push the river!   As someone who naturally strives and takes on many demands from a large family, I need to hear this advice often. These words have been a source of calm for my anxious mind and peace for my spirit. Rivers symbolise a natural flow and Taoist philosophy encourages us to align with life's inherent rhythms. In the Judeo-Christian narrative, rivers are central; they branch out in four directions to sustain the Garden of Eden in the creation story and the River of Life flows from the Divine throne to bring restoration in the biblical conclusion. Rivers embody life and energy, serving as a valuable metaphor for what it means to live a more surrendered existence.

To let things flow requires a surrender of control. People naturally desire to be in control, and, of course, we need to manage and organise things; otherwise, everything would be an almighty mess. Simply letting things happen can seem unappealing and weak. We can envision the defeated army surrendering to the conquerors or the overwhelmed mother who finds it easier to let her children do as they wish. Thus, there is a form of passive surrender that is unjust and unhealthy.

But there is a form of surrender that is healthy. Where we don't lose our potency and become defeated, hopeless or manipulative. This is choiceful surrender.

The surrender that we choose is anything but defeatist but rather courageous. It is not the same as submission imposed on us like we might imagine a Victorian husband who demands the obedience and submission of his wife, children and servants in his household. Choiceful surrender is about acceptance of realities we cannot change, and using our potency to choose a path where life flows around the problems.

Just like a boulder might rise up in the flow of a river and the water flowing around it is finding another way, so too our fluvial energy may at times encounter obstacles rising up within our own lives that we need to flow around. Our own lives have a flow, and obstacles will appear in their way, but like a river, we can accept difficulties and flow around the problems in our lives. My husband has learnt an amazing acceptance of his disabilities, and he is still positive and wants to live and do things that push the boundaries. I admire him.

My experience of James' disabilities feels like encountering a massive boulder in the flow of our lives that won't budge. Thus, I have adapted to navigate around these challenges. This has been a learning process filled with pain and frustration as I confront his difficulties, such as poor concentration, noise sensitivity, daily rest needs and an overall slower pace, among many others. However, I've come to understand that some obstacles are simply too significant to change this side of heaven and must be accepted as they are. Rather than fixating on the barriers that disrupt our journey, I have shifted my focus to the flow of life, where goodness and God exist, recognising that this flow ultimately cannot be obstructed.

The Serenity Prayer is a helpful way of understanding how to let the river of life flow.

"God grant me the serenity to accept the things I cannot change,

Courage to change the things I can,

And wisdom to know the difference."

The point of voluntarily surrendering to certain situations is that we can discover the Divine Flow of Life is greater than the obstacles. Achieving greater wholeness, sometimes surrendering to immovable boulders in our own lives and living in the flow of the Divine Life and surrendering to its transformative power, which surpasses all our challenges.

Practice

Read this, pausing to close your eyes and use your imaginative senses (visual, auditory, olfactory and any other sense) to engage as fully as possible in the experience.

See yourself sitting or standing next to a lovely stream or small river.

You can see the bed of different coloured pebbles and maybe some riverweed.

The water flows happily along, making bubbling sounds. The light reflects this flow of moving water. As you look downstream you see how individual small boulders rise out of the water. But how the water flows around them. You notice that some twigs and branches get caught in the shallows but how the water flows around them if it can't move them on.

Take a few pebbles from the riverbank, that symbolise your current struggles or concerns. Throw them one by one into the river surrendering them to the flow.

This could be a somatic prayer of releasing your worries into the Divine Flow who will hold them and whose flow is bigger than them.

Forgiveness

Forgiveness is the way we can surrender and let go in difficult relational situations.

Very recently, feeling riled by my child's insolent retort, the irritation amassed its potent presence to something more like outrage when I said they couldn't do something. After all I've done, I thought, compiling a mental list of how I've been wronged, and I felt a tsunami of rage gathering within my chest. Sadly, some of it came out, leading to a tension that took time to mend. Some anger is simply unhealthy, as it grips and controls us, potentially damaging people and relationships in its wake.

When people say they don't get angry, I don't believe them. It's like saying they don't breathe. To be human is to have access to the full range of emotions, and anger is one of them. There is healthy anger at the injustice of modern child slavery or anger at someone who carelessly cuts in front of us, almost causing a crash. Anger can provide energy for change and reform, and can also be an appropriate response when we are treated unfairly. We all experience anger over the many personal injustices we have faced. However, anger that is not acknowledged and processed becomes unhealthy. Unprocessed anger turns into bitterness and resentment, often manifesting as manipulation or subtle criticism. Whether we express or suppress our anger and resentment, we carry pain and anger in our hearts towards others, as life is broken.

I have discovered the power of letting go and forgiving as the most powerful antidote for my anger and resentment, largely because of the therapeutic benefits rather than the ethical dictates of the church. I need to forgive because I need peace in my heart instead of harbouring the toxic poison of resentment, anger and unforgiveness. There is a saying: "Unforgiveness is like drinking poison and hoping the other person dies." I sometimes view forgiveness less as a generous act of self-denial for the sake of others and more as an exercise in self-care that fosters peace and freedom.

Several years ago, I became aware of the unresolved resentment regarding my husband's disabilities and how they had affected my family and me. I have travelled around and through the different cycles of grief outlined by Kübler-Ross and reached a place of acceptance and surrender. One notable time of surrendering to the reality of grief and loss and relinquishing my resentment, I soon noticed the mild arthritis in my hands had completely disappeared. I've discovered a direct correlation between the sensitive pain in my hands and the extent to which I'm holding on to negative feelings. When I release people from my irritation or resentment, I not only notice my fists unfurling from their tense clench, but the arthritis also noticeably diminishes.

Perhaps some suppressed bitterness might be festering and hiding somewhere in your body, causing you pain. You could delve into your experience of pain, resentment and anger in particular circumstances and see if you can feel it as a specific somatic presence within you. Acknowledging these kinds of blockages in our inscape is both courageous and humble. However, to fully live in the flow of life, we must learn to forgive and let go. Forgiveness is rarely a one-time act; instead, it's a series of repeated choices made day after day and year after year with many people who upset us.

Forgiveness has two components. Firstly, we must acknowledge the pain we carry, as this is the root of the anger that has festered and become unhealthy. We can bravely delve into the core of our unforgiveness and acknowledge the unfairness, misunderstandings, abuse or violations we have experienced, allowing ourselves space to acknowledge and explore brokenness done unto us. If we pretend that our pain doesn't exist, we will cling to the splinter beneath the surface, preventing true healing from occurring. Only after this acknowledgement can we truly forgive and let go. While it may seem that the perpetrators escape unscathed, forgiveness ultimately liberates us. We forgive so that life can flow within us, around past offences and through us, facilitating our healing and wholeness.

Practice

Bring to mind someone you would like to practise forgiveness towards:

As you are aware of them, become aware of the hurt they have caused you. Acknowledge this pain giving it space. Maybe you can feel this in your body somewhere (uptight, constriction, heaviness, pain).

Then when you are ready, you can open and extend your hands as if you are physically letting go of something.

You could then also engage your exhale with the intention of letting go of the person or situation.

Do this several times slowly and with awareness and intention.

Receptivity

Attending secondary school away from home was often very lonely without my parents, and it taught me to be self-sufficient. The underlying message I absorbed from both my educational and cultural background was that self-sufficiency was the goal. It was essential to be independent, as this was supposedly a wonderful thing. However, completely shunning dependence on others can lead to feelings of isolation and burnout. Everyone relies on external resources; no person is an island.

Our inherent physical needs reveal our reliance on oxygen from the air, nutrients from our food and tap water. We are not independent. Beyond our need for water, food and air, we also require connections with others to avoid feelings of depression; ideally, this involves receiving their love and respect. Maslow's hierarchy of needs resembles a towering mountain, where our foundational physical needs pave the way to our ultimate existential needs. Every day, we strive to satisfy these needs in relation to the broader world. Consequently, being human implies being dependent, highlighting that receptivity is both intrinsic to human nature and vital for survival.

When James was first admitted to the hospital, my sense of self-sufficiency and agency disappeared overnight. I needed both grandmothers to help with the children and needed to find extra domestic help. I needed to buy readymade meals, and I needed money to help with these costs. I needed doctors and nurses for my husband's care and for them to update me about his condition; I needed emotional support from friends and strength from God. What I really didn't need was to strive towards more self-sufficiency, as I was overwhelmed and almost unable to cope. I needed to lean back and receive help from others.

"One should lie empty, open and choiceless like a beach—waiting for a gift from the sea," says Anne Morrow Lindbergh. Being receptive during times of crisis helps us weather the storms, but we would benefit from maintaining that openness in our everyday lives to uncover hidden gifts. When we are always doing and rarely being, when we are wilfully strong and self-sufficient, we miss the everyday gifts concealed in the life we are already living.

As I lift my head from my laptop right now, allowing myself to stop working, producing and achieving, I'm able to appreciate the symmetry of the windows that frame the beautiful trees and sky outside and I can hold the warm mug of coffee in both hands receiving the warmth as a gentle comfort.

This posture of receptivity has been vital to my spiritual journey. I have learnt to sit back and receive everyday gifts and the Divine Presence flowing through them. Rather than feeling that my spiritual life depends only on religious activity like petitionary prayer, reading my Bible, church fellowship or listening to worship music, I find deep nourishment in contemplative silence, simply being with the Divine without needing to say or do anything. The more I rest from my independence and activity and receive, the more I have to give to my family, friends and work. If we don't receive, our well runs dry, leaving us with little nourishment to offer others.

To be receptive is to be open to endless possibilities and to be resourced. Receptivity enables connections as others give to us and we can experience greater peace and fulfilment.

—— ⁓ ——

Practice

Christ on the cross gives us an image of vulnerability, surrender as well as offering and receptivity.:

Stand up and move your body into a posture of receptivity that feels right for you. You could perhaps take your arms wide, or somewhat open.

Perhaps you stand taller so your spine is not rounded, or even lift your head opening up the neck and shoulders and expanding the chest.

You might want to root your legs together or take them in a wider stance.

Play with the posture.

Breathe in fully as a reminder of your dependence on external sources for life, breath and everything else.

Notice how you feel in this more vulnerable and receptive posture. Are you able to embody the attitude even after returning to your normal tasks?

Gratitude

When we receive life's gifts with gratitude, our experience of life expands and we become more whole.

New shoes felt like an annual gift when I was young. We would visit the local Clarks store in the nearby town, where I would be fitted with a rather ordinary pair of black or navy shoes. I remember one year, around the age of nine when my mother allowed me to have a pair of black patent slip-ons; I placed them on the pillow next to my head, wanting them close to me as I slept. Perhaps you, too, can recall receiving something special as a child—something you treasured in a unique way.

Children are clearly dependent on receiving provisions and gifts, but the truth is, we all are. Everything is a gift. But to whom or what are we ultimately thankful? We did not create the world, others, or even ourselves. We did not form the stone that built our houses or the metal that made our cars. We did not create the nutrients in our food or the air we breathe. All of it is a gift. As the apostle Paul preached to a secular audience, "He himself gives everyone life and breath and everything else." This is both a statement of fact and of faith.

I remember the week before my wedding, a good friend, Clare, gave me a simple yet profound piece of advice: "Just thank God for everything—it will help you savour it." I took her words to heart, worried that the day would pass too quickly and leave me feeling as though I had barely experienced it. Her advice was invaluable. Practising gratitude allowed me to stop, linger and truly savour the details. This is the power of gratitude—it opens up space to fully receive and enjoy the gifts given to us in the moment.

Ann Voskamp, in her book 'One Thousand Gifts', explores this practice beautifully. She began listing everyday gifts in her life, reaching one thousand over several months. She taught me that gratitude is not reserved for life's high moments—like a wedding day —but is woven into the ordinary. The morning shadows stretch across the kitchen floor, inviting stillness. The warmth of sudsy dishwater turns a mundane task into a moment of presence. The curve of a child's smile, a fleeting connection of joy. Her reflections led me to realise that gratitude is not merely an antidote to a complaining spirit but a transformative, enriching practice.

Gratitude has been recognised as a therapeutic tool. As part of Social Prescribing in the NHS, some patients are encouraged to keep gratitude journals. Two recent clients of mine adopted this practice, and both found it significantly aided their healing from anxiety and depression. Gratitude anchors us in the present moment, revealing the hidden gifts of everyday life.

Beyond its emotional benefits, gratitude shifts our perspective. It redirects our focus from the metaphorical one black dot in the middle of a white piece of paper, allowing us to recognise the goodness around us. It reorients our narrative—from seeing ourselves as victims of hardship to acknowledging the blessings we receive. Practising gratitude enables us to experience greater presence, richness and beauty in our daily lives, helping us to live more fully.

Gratitude also deepens relationships. When we receive a toddler's colourful drawing or a friend's thoughtful gift, we naturally thank them, strengthening our connection. Gifts signify love and a desire for connection, and our gratitude nurtures that bond. The same is true in our relationship with the Giver of All Life—when we express gratitude to the Creator, we find our connection to Him strengthened in a profound and life-giving way.

There are so many gifts of beauty, goodness and love hidden in the everyday, waiting to be noticed. If we slow down and create space to perceive them, our view of ourselves, others, the world and the Divine expands, and we can experience greater peace and fulfilment.

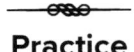

Practice

Breathe a little more deeply to settle yourself.

Each in-breath is a gift of life. Breathe in the gift of being alive and give thanks.

Then bring to mind ten things, counting them off on your fingers, that you are grateful for. You can choose the big things like health, and the small things, the birdsong you noticed on your walk.

Practice this each day for a week if you wish.

Chapter 10

Nurturing Growth

Growing into wholeness is healthy, but a drive to grow our achievements can be unhealthy.

There is immense pressure on us today to perform and achieve, whether it is in the domestic or public sphere. Our culture seems to prioritise productivity and growth as the supreme measure of how valuable we are. We are under pressure to increase our social media following, boost our bank accounts or expand our businesses. These relentless demands are draining us and attacking us on multiple levels, along with our children and the environment, where the message of more, more, more is unrelenting. Such overwhelming demands can sometimes feel like a form of bondage to a master we cannot see and who does not have our best interests.

This oppression of the productivity and growth model seems to be internalised by us, leading to self-imposed pressure to achieve more effectively enslaving ourselves to these dictates without even realising it. Much like the proverbial frog slowly boiled alive, we often fail to notice it until it is too late. This pressure dehumanises us and, I suggest, is largely responsible for the high levels of stress, anxiety and depression prevalent today. We have strayed too far in one direction and urgently need to seek peace and balance.

The pathway to wholeness emphasizes growth but in a unique manner. Instead of simply doing more, striving for greater achievements and chasing seemingly impossible goals, we must reframe this idea to tap into the hidden wisdom present in women's experiences. Rather than focusing solely on production, we should nurture what we already have. Women have historically been tasked with the roles of nurturing and caregiving, looking after children, supporting the sick or aiding the elderly, while men have more often engaged in public activity. Women might be more inclined to attend to the needs of others, teaching us the crucial value of resilience and the growth that stems from nurturing. Consider the distress faced by some children due to neglect or abuse; the lack of nurturing during their formative years can severely hinder their resilience and development.

We need to cultivate a nurturing approach towards ourselves. Many of us feel inadequate, ashamed or overwhelmed and extending acceptance and compassion towards ourselves helps us find healing and wholeness. Jesus teaches that the second most important thing in life is to "love others as you love yourself." I have personally found self-compassion to be a powerful tool for transformation in my life and in the lives of my clients. As we practice self-acceptance and self-love, we empower ourselves to flourish and grow, allowing us to offer more love to others as well.

Self-acceptance

Self-acceptance can feel like failure, but is the beginning of success. We might look in the mirror and wish we saw something different, not content with what is before us. Our homes and our careers can come under the same scrutiny, as can our social lives, schedules and even our children's lives. This pursuit of growth and improvement drives us to seek beyond our current boundaries, aiming for ever-higher standards. However, this quest can be both exhausting and disappointing.

Sometimes, we must reach our breaking point or dive into deep disappointment before we can let go of unhelpful attitudes and patterns and embrace a new approach. Living in a healthier, more fulfilling way involves realising that you are already enough. I know it sounds clichéd, but without this realisation, we tend to live in insecurity seeking validation of our significance and self-worth from other's approval or from our accomplishments. What happens when we don't receive the accolades our egos crave, or when those around us are unavailable or uninterested in celebrating our achievements? We end up feeling uncertain and fragmented. We are already good enough and we can uncover the treasures hidden within our current lives so we become more whole.

"There is nobody like you, and since the beginning, there has never been anyone like you. No one has the same smile, eyes, hands or hair. No one owns your handwriting or your voice. Nobody has your taste for food or music or dances or draws like you.

You are unique. You are entirely different from anyone who has ever lived on the earth—the only one in the world with your particular abilities. Whilst there will always be someone better than you at one thing or another, nobody in the universe possesses the unique combination of your talents, feelings, thoughts and ways of being. Throughout all of the time, nobody will ever walk, talk or think exactly like you do. You are a rare being, and rarity holds enormous value. So, because you have such great value, simply by being yourself, there is no need to imitate anyone else; in fact, this would create a flaw within you. There is a special purpose for you to play in this world, and nobody else is qualified to play this role. Only you are qualified. You are unique; you are special; you are of ultimate value." (Paraphrased from 'You're Special'—Anonymous).

How we see life and how we see ourselves is very important. If we see ourselves as unique and valuable, then we will nurture the gift of our own being. If we see life as something to be experienced and enjoyed rather than to produce and consume, we will live a healthier life and bless others along the way. To see ourselves as a valuable presence within the world is not selfish or arrogant; so often, self-centredness arises from the desire to be more and have more because we don't believe we are of value. Nurturing the good and the Divine Image already present within us is a way of seeing and recognising the treasure invested in each of us, releasing us from the futile pursuit of acquisition and admiration.

How we see ourselves is key. We need to be aware of who we are and humbly surrender to the beauty and blessing we are invested in. By accepting who we are, we can cease from striving and come to greater peace and flourishing and this is true success.

Practice

Placing both hands over your heart and gently say, I accept myself and I am enough.

Repeat this several times with pauses.

You could try this mantra: breathe in I and breathe out am enough. As you say these words, you engage in a deeper exhale.

Notice how your body feels during and after this process.

Remember that it is not about trying hard to think better but rather about surrendering to the truth that you are valuable.

Self-compassion

When we are full of pain and brokenness, what we need to give ourselves most is self-compassion.

Give yourself some grace, I would regularly say to Cara, who came to see me because of her emotional outbursts. She explained that sometimes she couldn't hold it together, and when her partner placed excessive demands on her, her self-control gave way to turbulent torrents of tears and ranting and raving about how awful she was and her life was, and she wanted help to stop these outbursts. Our curious enquiry together into the deeper workings of her life revealed a history of trauma. Absent and sick parents who needed her emotional and practical support, several years of sexual abuse then the self-abuse of anorexia, workaholism and excessive exercise. It didn't surprise me in the slightest that she might flip her lid occasionally, but the healing came bit by bit as she learnt to live the refrain Give yourself some grace. By learning to engage in self-compassion, this beautiful woman found some healing and began to live a more peaceful and flourishing life.

Self-compassion is not a luxury; it's a necessity. Kristin Neff has become a leading teacher on the benefits of self-compassion and explains that it is necessary to face life's inevitable struggles. My own findings as a friend and therapist are that many people, especially women, tend towards a merciless self-judgement that cripples. "With self-compassion, we give ourselves the same kindness and care we'd give to a good friend," advises Neff, as she continues to explain that "self-compassion opens our heart in a way that can transform our lives."

Self-compassion aids the cleansing process so we become more whole. When we acknowledge the brokenness that has appeared in our life due to ourselves or others, we need to accept and be kind to ourselves. Bringing harsh judgement down on ourselves with our internal critic who is ever-present, only makes us feel more ashamed. We then retreat and hide from ourselves and others, afraid of indeed being seen, and so live only half-alive rather than fully alive. The Bible even teaches that it is the "kindness of God that leads to repentance", and so kindness to oneself is something to cultivate to live a whole and holy life.

I realise that I am a carer, not only to my children, who are now flying the nest, but increasingly to my husband, whose medical profile has become more complex and disabling. When I struggle with the demands that disability presents, I realise I have a choiceful surrender by also engaging in self-compassion which really helps this. I can listen to my internal struggle due to the limitations and needs that disability brings, showing myself some compassion as I acknowledge, accept and then let go. This enables me to find peace, and I have become more resilient over the years as a result. Self-compassion has become profoundly healing for me, meaning that I don't have to exile the uncomfortable parts of myself but can bring them to the light, experiencing the whole of myself, allowing the unattractive aspects to be accepted and transformed and to experience greater peace and wholeness amid the struggles.

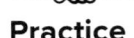

Practice

Neff teaches these three steps you could practice, especially during moments of self-judgement or difficulty.

Notice and name your experience without judgement, e.g. This is stress, this feels painful, I'm feeling overwhelmed.

Remind yourself that you are not alone; this struggle is part of a shared human experience. For example, other people feel like this too or pain and disappointment are part of being human.

Offer yourself kindness, comfort or reassurance, even placing a hand on your heart or a self-hug, saying, I can give myself some grace right now, I can forgive and love myself in this place, or all things shall be well. Speak to yourself as you would to a friend.

Rooted and Peaceful

Self-acceptance and self-compassion enable us to feel grounded and at peace. We stop growing physically by about eighteen or thereabout. The adult human has then completed the task of physical growth, and the task of living is about settling into the life we are already living. We find this same pattern in the life of a tree. Take the common oak tree, which can live for up to 1,000 years. The initial

100 years involve rapid height growth, and thereafter, the oak shifts its energy to developing a deeper root system, a strong, resilient trunk and flourishing branches and foliage. Our friend Simon was out walking when James was first in hospital and he relayed to us how he had come across a tree by a local river whose roots were exposed. The roots were a complex weave, and he said it reminded him of my husband's roots of faith and character and he believed it would enable James to weather the storm. I agree with this picture, and my husband's resilience is partly due to his being rooted in the Divine.

Roots enable stability. Being rooted or grounded as a person is to experience peace. Attachment theory in psychology explains how a person's childhood experience of connection, security and security provides them with a foundation to support them and help them know acceptance and peace in their lives. When this is absent people can grow up with anxious, avoidant or disorganised styles of relating and being. Whilst we might not have had the ideal childhood we are able to heal and experience peace and security in adulthood by practising self-acceptance and self-compassion. Peace comes from acceptance rather than judgement. We can start by accepting ourselves, including our pain, brokenness and mistakes. This acceptance is not passive but offers a foundation of peace that allows us to grow.

We can find security and peace by having a narrative that is bigger than ourselves, a philosophical or spiritual narrative. I have personally found peace in the rich heritage of the ancient Christian tradition; my faith has been a profound source of nourishment for me. It enabled me to embrace a comforting refrain when I felt utterly fragmented in 2012: Whatever happens, it will be okay. This assurance stemmed from a broader, deeper trust that the Divine was supporting me and my family and assured me that everything would ultimately serve the greater good. The promise of heavenly renewal filled me with hope. Although my husband has not been healed and we continue to face challenges, I mostly maintain my peace, as I am anchored in a foundation far larger and more stable than myself.

To have an enduring peace we need a meaning far bigger than ourselves. A pathway to wholeness is built on solid foundations underpinned by the Divine who offers a "peace that passes all understanding," (Philippians) for those who travel upon it.

Practice

Lie down on the ground. Feet falling outwards, arms by your side with palms facing upwards, eyes closed.

Feel the points of contact your body has with the ground.

Take five deeper breaths, fully exhaling before allowing your breath to settle into its own rhythm.

Unbrace any tense muscles.

Acknowledge and accept any pain or discomfort physically (as well as mentally and emotionally).

Allow yourself to sink into the ground.

Invite peace, the presence of peace to be with you, under you and holding you.

Strong and Resilient

Resilience is something of a buzzword in the educational world. It also swims around in the wellness world, and yet rarely do people explain how we are meant to be resilient beyond simply being told to be. Neuropsychologist and meditation teacher Rich Hanson describes it like this, "Resilience is the capacity to recover from adversity, adapt to change, and keep going in the face of hardship. It's not about never falling—it's about learning how to rise." To be resilient is to be strong; to be able to weather storms like a tree in a hurricane or a boat in a gale and it is learnt amid struggle and suffering.

Being resilient means recognising challenges, pain and loss and accepting them instead of denying their existence. Resilience is developed by enduring hardships and understanding that we are greater than our struggles. If we can move beyond these difficulties, we are indeed more than the challenges we face. With each obstacle we overcome, we strengthen ourselves and we become resilient.

What have you come through?

Right now you are here. You have survived.

Having a sense of yourself, that you are a real human being with a real body, with real emotions that you experience, all contribute to a sense of self. Nurturing somatic awareness—that we are a body—roots us in the present moment, reminding us that we are alive and not utterly overwhelmed or extinguished. This awareness enables us to realise we already have strength and resilience hidden within us. We increase our resilience by increasing our sense of self—that we still are in the face of challenge. I discovered this somatically and spiritually through running a marathon. We can know this simply by the fact we have overcome many challenges and are still alive and kicking. Increasing your awareness of your physical self is resourceful for resilience, so practising breath awareness, engaging your five senses more regularly, or doing body scans or mindful exercise are all powerful ways of increasing your resilience.

Resilience can also be cultivated through enhanced spiritual awareness. Focusing solely on our problems can lead to feelings of being overwhelmed. However, by embracing a greater narrative that transcends our individual experiences and provides meaning, we can discover peace and strength. Recent decades have seen a noticeable decline in traditional religion, along with a growing interest in spirituality, which I understand. Yet, engaging in a purely self-constructed spirituality can expose us to vulnerabilities, as it leans heavily on our personal interpretations. Even if we gather diverse belief systems from various sources, we remain the curators, which may lack the depth of a tested, reliable narrative. I suggest that the way of Jesus offers an ultimately dependable and resilient pathway that leads us toward wholeness.

The way of Jesus describes how the Divine became fully human living an everyday life with a physical body, experiencing struggle and suffering just as we do. Jesus lived a holistic life where his body and soul were always and forever integrated. He lived a surrendered yet highly potent life with no trace of striving or stress. The actual life of Jesus is a symbol of beauty rising out of suffering, and if our roots are in this narrative ground, then we have access to the same peace and resilience that he modelled.

The journey towards wholeness rests on the steadfast narrative and life of Jesus, the Divine-Human, providing us with a solid foundation to cultivate peace and strength in our daily lives.

Practice

Seated or lying down, adopt a posture cf openness, maybe arms open, palms upturned, chest uplifted. Shift around and make this posture your own.

Notice your breath, taking a few deeper breaths.

Then, letting the breath settle, say in a quiet whisper or in the quiet of your mind:

"Come" on the inhale, "Lord Jesus" on the exhale.

Simply be open, and curious, inviting the reality of Jesus' presence to be with you.

Do you notice anything after a few minutes of this practice? There is no right or wrong answer.

Flourishing and Fulfilled

Flourishing and fulfilment are our intended Divine birthright.

I find it difficult not to challenge three topics that are current in the culture around me; three interrelated things: preachers whose only focus is directing their audiences to what they should be doing, the secular concept of self-realisation as the ultimate goal in life and the idea that we need to be healed just so we can help others. I believe these ideals, whilst having good intentions, can limit genuine human flourishing to something that is a less wholesome experience. But my shadow side that triggers has obviously tried to find meaning by doing all of the above! I will unpack why they might be common beliefs and how they stand in the way of true flourishing.

Firstly, being told what we should do to be a better person does not enable wholeness. It is like being prodded in the back to keep on walking when you are thirsty and exhausted, rather than being allowed to rest. We are foremost human beings, not human doings. Secondly, self-realisation so often just ends with self and provides us with nothing to be grounded in beyond our self. The self and nothing but the self is a lonely and limiting experience; there is a much greater realm, a Divine realm that we can connect to. Thirdly, we don't just get healed to rush out and help others, who will then go and help others, who will help others and so on and the merry dance continues. At some point, the buck needs to stop with our own experience, where we can know healing and wholeness for ourselves.

To flourish and find fulfilment is to be inspired towards something greater, just like the branches of the tree extend outwards. It is not about doing more or being more, but being who we are truly meant to be. We need to have a vision of something transcendent that enables us to go beyond our mere self to become more whole. The patient who lies in a windowless room is less likely to heal as quickly as the patient who can look out of her hospital window at green trees and blue skies and hear birdsong. When we have a vision of beauty that exists beyond us, it calls forth the healing and wholeness within us. When we find some measure of healing and health we are to celebrate and nurture it, like the biblical story of the woman who threw a party when she found her lost coin. So much of our wholeness is lost to us amid everyday demands, and when we find this health and wholeness, we need to nurture and enjoy it alongside helping others on their journey.

The fulfilling life we desire is concealed within our current existence. Upon uncovering these hidden treasures, we should pause, appreciate and celebrate instead of rushing to achieve more. The journey to wholeness excavates the wealth within our lives, encouraging us to bloom where we are planted. Just like a magnificent tree, true fulfilment comes from deepening our roots in nourishing soil and strengthening our core, enabling us to reach upwards and outwards. This connection with others, the world and the Divine allows us to unfold our essence and thrive in the life we inhabit.

So often, we enslave ourselves to oppressive rules that drive us, and we fail to permit ourselves to enjoy life. There are two internal oppositions to enjoying our life at both ends of the spectrum: envy and guilt. Which one is the draw for yourself? Like many others, guilt is my natural inclination, and in the past I have felt apologetic for my blessings, thinking I need to deny myself and strive to do more and be better. Permitting myself to enjoy my life has been none other than enlivening. I am able to find joy in the life I have despite the problems and challenges. There will always be someone who appears to have a more flourishing life than ours leading to envy, and there will be others who seem to experience a worse life than ourselves, giving way to guilt. But permitting ourselves to enjoy our own life will enable us to flourish just as each of us longs to.

Irenaeus, a theologian from the second century, stated, "The glory of God is a person fully alive." If we interpret this to mean that being fully alive glorifies the Creator, we can free ourselves from guilt. Flourishing and fulfilment are the Divine birthright bestowed upon us by the Creator.

Jesus said that he had come to bring each of us life

and life in all its fullness. There is permission and promise in these words. As we practise becoming more whole we will find that it is a pathway of enjoyment in the everyday. Will we surrender to this possibility and permit ourselves to enjoy our lives?

Practice

Settle yourself physically and take some breaths to calm.

Meditate on these words of Jesus:

Read—"I have come to give you life and life in all its fullness."

Reflect—"I have come to give you life and life in all its fullness."

Respond—"I have come to give you life and life in all its fullness."

Receive—"I have come to give you life and life in all its fullness"

OLIVIA SHONE

Conclusion

The pathway to wholeness ends where it started. It's within the life you are already living that you find the life you long for.

We inhabit a challenging and broken world where daily pressures accumulate, causing stress, struggle and suffering that leave us feeling overwhelmed, disconnected and unfulfilled. Yet, there is still hope for transcending a merely "*bios*" existence of "survival" to embrace the "*zōē*" life of "fullness and flourishing."

The opportunity to experience wholeness, greater peace and fulfilment, is hidden in the everyday and within ourselves. We need to shift our perspective from believing that this lies beyond our grasp to realising that the point and meaning of our lives are within us and are very much in our grasp. As we explore the inscapes of our own life and the everyday things we can find the hidden treasure of experiencing wholeness which is an experience of peace, resilience and fulfilment.

The pathway to becoming whole is suggested in the experiences women have had throughout time and place. Women have commonly experienced silence and suffering and have wisdom to offer us all. As we bring a redemptive lens to women's experiences, we find a framework of wisdom that guides us on this pathway.

This framework explores two often neglected dimensions

of human existence: the somatic and spiritual. Shifting perspective away from treating our mental and emotional issues by only addressing our thoughts and emotions brings a more holistic aspect to healing. Current studies on somatic awareness, in conjunction with the enduring tradition of Christian spirituality, serve as valuable resources. Together, these two dimensions complement one another, providing us with both spiritual physicality and an embodied spirituality in daily life.

To begin the journey to wholeness, we need to slow down and find stillness and space to restore ourselves and start savouring life. Wholeness involves richly experiencing our lives, which cannot be fully grasped through intellectual knowledge. By engaging our innate capacities for intuition, along with somatic and spiritual sensing, we can explore the symbols, stories and lessons of everyday life to reconnect with ourselves and the world around us.

Our bodies are sacred, as is the everyday, where graces unfold that enhance our spiritual experience of life. We can identify symbolic connections between our physical and spiritual realities, enabling us to address fundamental existential needs through our embodied experiences. Consequently, holistic spirituality intertwines the material world with the Divine realm. We discover that a bond with the earth, its inhabitants, beauty and bounty also fosters a deeper connection with the Creator.

This deeper, broader and more holistic experience of life also grounds us during times of stress, struggle and suffering. Wholeness does not deny or shy away from harsh realities but confronts them head-on. As we continue on the path to living in wholeness, we find we can journey around or through suffering, revealing a presence and power greater than any difficulty we may face. We discover that we can experience wholeness despite and sometimes even through the brokenness in the world. There is a paradox that as we surrender, we are not overwhelmed by life's struggles and sufferings, but rather we are reconnected to ourselves, to the world around us and also to God. We find the hidden places, the mundane everyday and even our struggles and sufferings, are the very places where we might nurture a growing wholeness.

This pathway to becoming whole is found in practical and physical things which lead us into an experience of the spiritual and sublime. We do not find it by more effort and activity but through acceptance and surrender. Surrender not only enables us to receive and savour the beauty and blessing of creation and Creator but enables connection with self and others. As we admit our own vulnerabilities and forgive the brokenness of others we can reconnect with ourselves, others and the Other. Living whole means we can perceive beauty in everything—people and planet—that invites a connection with Ultimate Beauty, or the Divine, which is a holy thing.

May you continue to journey upon this pathway until the day you become healed, healthy and holy whole.

OLIVIA SHONE

About PublishU

PublishU enables you to tell your story or communicate your message by writing and publishing a book worldwide.

"I never thought I would be able to write a book, let alone in 100 days… now I'm asking what else have I told myself that I can't do that I actually can?'"

PublishU Author

To find out more visit

www.PublishU.com

OLIVIA SHONE

Printed in Dunstable, United Kingdom